Holistic Education and Yoga

Holistic Education and YOGA

Neelam Sharma

SP SHIPRA
SHIPRA

Rs. 180; US$ 9

ISBN: 978-93-86262-24-0

First Published in India in 2017

Holistic Education and Yoga

Published by:
SHIPRA PUBLICATIONS
LG 18-19, Pankaj Central Market
I.P. Ext., Patparganj, Delhi 110092, India
Tel.: +91 11 2223 5152/6152
E-mail: info@shiprapublication.com
www.shiprapublication.com

स्वामी विवेकानन्द योग-अनुसन्धान-संस्थानम्

Swami Vivekananda Yoga Anusandhāna Samsthānam

(Declared as Deemed-to-be University under Section 3 of the UGC Act, 1956)

Eknath Bhavan, # 19, Gavipuram Circle, Kempegowda Nagar,
Bangalore - 560 019

Ph: 080 - 2661 2669, Telefax: 080 - 2660 8645

E-mail: svyasa@svyasa.edu.in Website: www.svyasa.edu.in

Foreword

It is a great pleasure to write this foreword for the book titled 'Holistic Education and Yoga'. Although this is a maiden effort of the author Dr. Neelam Sharma, it is an appreciable work.

As Swami Vivekananda said, "Anything that is secret and mysterious in these systems of Yoga should be at once rejected". The author has researched extensively from various texts to offer a comprehensive unbiased overview on the subject of Holistic Development of a human being, unveiling whatever may be looked upon as secrets. Yoga is the art and science of union and should be easily taught to and learnt by every student for their holistic development.

I am truly hopeful that this book will be quite helpful to the readers, teachers, students and researchers. The author's compilation of different research material and her personal research clearly present her keen inclination, dedication and missionary zeal towards this task. With this tenacity and scientific rigour, I am certain that we can look forward to many more writings from her. I am glad that her cutting-edge research methodology developed during her Doctorate in Yoga at S-VYASA is bearing fruit in the form of these writings.

I wish Dr. Neelam Sharma success in her new venture.

With Love,

नागेन्द्र

Dr. H.R. Nagendra
President: VYASA
Chancellor: S-VYASA

20/10/2016
Delhi

Preface

Man is the supreme creation engraved by the Almighty. All knowledge is potentially there in the human mind, but it needs a proper education to explore and draw it out. Ancient Indian education system is focussed on holistic education. It involves a harmonious blending of the knowledge of the outer world (*avidya*) and inner world (*vidya*). And Maharishi Patanjali, a mystic, blessed us with a divine knowledge named 'Yoga'.

Today, the world is full of stress and unhealthy competition where a woman/man runs from pillar to post in search of boundless happiness throughout her/his life. S/he ultimately feels exhausted with no happiness in her/his account and as a result faces depression, anxiety and other psycho-somatic problems. Moreover, our present education system, burdened with a variety of aims and objectives (theoretically), fails to equip our students with certain life skills which could have enabled them to face realities of life with vigour and vitality. An utmost need of the time is that we must go back to our ancient texts to get right directions for our adolescents, who are almost confused, defocused and lost in the virtual world. Such an education is required that may help the learner to be with her/his inner self, which may guide her/him to lead a balanced life, and assist to drive positive and constructive energy from her/his inner source to counter the challenges of life. Dissatisfied, frustrated, unhappy and unhealthy youth cannot build a healthy and happy nation. The synthesis of education and yoga is one of the effective tool to make harmonious and holistic development of the learners.

This book highlights the treasure which our ancient scholars have gifted us. Yoga is the state of inner tranquillity, mastery over mind and freedom from fears and anxieties. It is a science that works holistically to strengthen the inner being. This maiden writing is an endeavour to present a resource book for all the students, teachers and research scholars, who are rightly into the field of yoga and education. It may help them to unfold different dimensions of yoga which can be used to make their task accomplished at a satisfaction level.

The book is the outcome of an extensive discussions with yoga experts, school faculty and students. It opens with the concept of Holistic Education and unfolds its further details. The best possible efforts are made to provide thorough understanding on holistic education, yoga, stress, academic performance, memory, concentration and intelligence. In addition, a summary of my research project, wherein 'value orientation programme and yoga module' is discussed, added here enhances value of the book. All possible efforts are made to use simple and effective language corresponding to the explanation of the content.

I convey my sincere feelings of indebtedness to Dr. H.R. Nagendra, (fondly called 'Guru Ji'), the Chancellor of Swami Vivekananda Yoga Anusandhana Samasthana (SVYASA) for support and guidance to accomplish the research project.

I extend my heartfelt gratitude to the eminent scholars and authors whose work has provided illustrious guidelines in the preparation of this book. I also thank Mr. D. Kumar, Shipra Publications, for reposing faith in me. I have no hesitation to own the responsibility of any error or omission in my endeavour. The readers' suggestions are welcomed.

Dr. Neelam Sharma

Contents

List of Tables and Figures

LIST OF TABLES

LIST OF FIGURES

1
Holistic Education

Man is the top creation of Almighty. He is endowed with ultimate freedom—freedom of choice. He is encountered with a variety of choices during his life time; beginning from birth till his last breath. For human beings, this freedom of choice is also the biggest challenge. The journey of actions depends on the choices a person makes. Education enables the individual to grow by making right choices. Education being an emphatic social activity, is a voyage from 'womb to tomb'.

Having traversed a long journey from ancient to present era, education has all along been defined by various scholars. Review of the definitions of education concludes that the process of education must take into consideration some key factors like the individual and society. An individual being a part of the society is impacted by it and in turn also influences the society by his behaviour. In order to create a humanistic society, the innate potentialities of the individual need to be drawn out to make him a complete man.

Man has two facets: spiritual and material. He is the sum total of body, mind and spirit. Vedanta believes that the essence of man lies in his soul, which he possesses in addition to his body and mind. Swami Vivekananda describes education as a process to manifest the divinity already existing in man. Education is not the amount of information that is put into the brain of a learner which may remain undigested. Education is an ongoing activity, by which character is formed, strength of mind is increased and intellect is sharpened. Education enables a person to stand on his feet by making the right choices. Anything related with divinity is as pure and perfect as the divine Himself. All knowledge, powers are within. All secrets of nature and force are also within. Right educational environment is required to draw out the hidden treasures for an all-round development of a child.

Self-activity and self-effort of the learner are the jewels to be worn within. Physically fit body, an unwavering mind and sparkling spirit are the abundant treasures of an individual. Swami Vivekananda dreamt of an education which would develop character, brings unity in diversity and help the seeker to realize the 'self' in order to attain the ultimate aim of life. No system or philosophy of education can be perfect, if it is single-tracked, aiming either for material prosperity or for spiritual upliftment. The synthesis of the three—*dharma* (religion), *artha* (material prosperity), *kama* (desire)—is vital for the overall development of human personality. Holistic education aims at an all-round development of an individual's personality.

The educationists today are in a state of dilemma as to what kind of education would be best suited in the present context. Since the world is passing through a flux of socio-politico-economic changes, a significant role of education is required to fulfil the existing demands of the society and the growing challenges of the new era. Mahatma Gandhi emphasised upon the *seven dangers to humanity*:

- Wealth without work
- Pleasure without conscience
- Knowledge without character
- Business without ethics
- Science without humanity
- Religion without sacrifice
- Politics without principle

Education is needed to produce such individuals who are connected to their inner selves. The real challenge facing the educational system is to establish students in their value system, both outwardly and inwardly. To achieve this objective, love for culture, human goodness, respect for nature and concern for flora and fauna must be part of the scheme of education. A multi-faceted development of an individual's personality—physical, mental, moral and spiritual—can be achieved through proper education. What is required today is to reorganise and reshape the education system to facilitate actualization of the self. Holistic education can go a long way to accomplish the desired objective of complete human development.

Meaning of Holistic Education

The word 'Holistic' is derived from the word 'Holism' (Greek' *holos'*) , meaning 'all, whole, entire'. This means that any system should be viewed as a whole and not as a collection of its parts. A human being is an integrated unit which is comprised of body, mind and spirit. For evaluation of the performance of a student in any field, there is need to assess him/her as a whole individual and not as a fragmented entity in compartmentalised form.

It was J C Smuts, who coined the term Holism in his first publication 'Holism and Evolution' (1926). He opined that Holism is a concept that represents the entire (whole) universe. Holism attributes another theory to the concept of the universe, different from materialistic or spiritualistic explanations. According to the Holism theory, the ultimate reality in the universe is not defined by matter or spirit but by the concept of a whole. While offering this new definition, Smuts clearly opined that its primary and proper use was to denote the totality of wholes which operate as real factors and gives to reality its dynamic evolutionary creative character.

Man is a social animal and he recognizes his identity through his interaction and connection with the society. He learns about values, relations, inert-relations, physical nature and surroundings by being a part of the social system. Family too is a miniature form of society, where he starts his initial experiences and captures his learning diary of early childhood. The term holistic education is often used to refer to the more democratic and humanistic type of alternative education. Holistic education is different than other forms of education in a way that its goals, learning experiences and its focus on value system are more specific and deeply rooted.

Holistic education focuses on the fullest possible development of the person, encouraging individuals to become the very best or finest that they can be and enabling them to experience all they can from life and reach their goals.

In other words, Holistic Education aims at the following:

- Growth of every person's intellectual, emotional, social, physical, artistic, creative and spiritual potential.
- Nurtures healthy and curious persons who wish to learn and are also receptive to new learning.

Ancient Indian View of Holistic Education

The aim of ancient Indian education was to develop the mind and soul of the man. It stressed on the empowering of human potential which in turn would lead them towards becoming a complete human being. It further focused on strengthening of value based culture, discipline and humanitarian attitude of the society. It was always in favour of inculcating universal qualities which would not hamper human values such as dignity, perseverance, honesty, trust, and encourage students for working towards common welfare of the society as a whole. Basically ancient education system aimed at character formation through proper coordination of theory with practice. The role of a teacher was very important. The teacher was expected to inculcate values in the students by narrating the stories of heroes from epics and ancient history. They were also expected to narrate the stories of great valour of eminent personalities living in their own times. It had the mission to create a society of individuals with strong character, living a life of contentment.

The objectives of ancient education were summarized in a triple formula which gave a wide and lofty framework to the ancient system of education:

> 'asato ma sadgamaya
> tamaso ma jyotirgamaya
> mrityorma amritam gamaya'
> Lead me from falsehood to truth
> Lead me from darkness to light
> Lead me from death to immortality
>
> —*Brihadaranyaka Upanishad, I.3.28*

Our ancient masters believed in an education which would bring wisdom. They focussed on trinity of Truth, Immortality and Light—interwoven together. True knowledge brings light (wisdom). It was thought that this light would enable the learner to attain the stage of immortality.

Ancient education system also aimed for self-realization, and the students were provided a congenial environment wherein they could live with the thought 'I am Braham'. It went beyond the personal ego. The students were made to believe in and realize their full potential, to merge into super-soul, i e Braham. It was a holistic education, which was a fine combination of the knowledge of inner world (*vidya*) and that of outer world (*avidya*). There was a consistent effort to maintain harmony of both these worlds. The education system was evolved in a way that could help the students to lead exemplary lives.

This system of education also aimed at creating a mind which is both rational and sensitive; with a sense of appreciation, aesthetics, humility and awareness of its limitations. On the other hand, it is enquiring, logical, believing in experimentation.

Modern Indian View of Holistic Education

Various philosophers and educationists defined education in a comprehensive manner, which is the replica of holistic education.

In Guru Nanak's view, education aims to uplift the downtrodden, serve the sufferers, reform the treacherous, and realise the divine within.

Mahatma Gandhi defines education as an all-round drawing out of the best in child and man—body, mind and spirit.

Rabindranath Tagore remarked that education leads to harmony of life with all existence and thus enables the mind to find out that ultimate truth which gives the wealth of inner light, love and significance to life.

Dr Zakir Hussain viewed education as a process of the individual mind, capable of achieving the best possible development. It begins from the time of birth and continues till the last moment of death.

Western View of Holistic Education

Holistic Education moves with a specific aim for the complete development of the individual by channelizing his whole potential to make him a fully developed human being. It endeavours to utilise the theory of 'inter-relations and inter-connections' whether it is in pedagogy, subject matter, scholastic cum non-scholastic activities. John Dewey talked about tri-polar nature of education, which means that education is a process which involves teacher, student and social environment. Whole curriculum of education is based on social environment and society is an outcome of interconnectedness. Holistic education too aims at relationship between the whole and the part. It strives to limelight the strong connection of part with the whole; man with the society; man with the nation; man with the world, man with the cosmos; man with the eternity and man with his 'self' (Table 1.1).

Miller (1991) has proposed that education may be described as holistic when it exemplifies the following characteristics:

- nurtures the broad development of the students and focuses on their intellectual, emotional, social, physical, creative or intuitive, aesthetic and spiritual potentials.
- promotes the importance of relationships at all levels within a learning community in which the educator and student work together in an open and collaborative relationship.
- emphasises on life experience and learning beyond the confines of the classroom and the formal educational environment towards education as growth, discovery and a broadening of horizons. It encourages a desire to elicit meaning and understanding and to engage with the world.
- empowers learners to examine critically the cultural, moral and political contexts of their lives. It leads learners towards actively challenging and changing cultural values to meet human needs.

UNESCO (1996) states that there is an emphasis on a broad educational approach that addresses the intellectual, personal and interpersonal development of students, and puts in place many of the values, attitudes and skills that will serve them well throughout life. Such a broad development cannot be claimed by the knowledge-laden education systems that have dominated for so many years. It brings closer the realization of 'learning to be' and 'learning to live together' that have been identified in the Delor's report.

Table 1.1: Evolution of the Holistic Education

Period (Century)	*Dominant ideas*	*Implications for schooling*
17th-19th	Scientific Enlightenment—materialistic, positivistic, epistemology	Traditional schooling; teacher-centred
19th-20th	Materialism—objectivity	
19th-20th	Capitalism—Product efficiency	
18th/19th	Romantics	Child-centred, personal growth
1830s	Transcendentalists	
1910s/1920s	Progressive educators	Whole person
Early 20th	Eastern and perennial philosophies; new physics; ecosystems	New paradigms, alternative Epistemology
1960s/1970s	Holistic and systems theories; Counter cultures (Women's Movement, Environmental Movement, New Age Movement, Multiculturism); Critics of modernism; Radical educators; New epistemological perspectives; Deep Ecology, Indigenous Wisdom, Spirituality, Transpersonal Psychology, The Feminine, Cosmology, Perennial Philosophies, Eastern Philosophy	Interconnectedness, new paradigms, alternative epistemologies; context/subjectivity; social justice, dialogue
1970s/1980s	Humanistic psychology, Humanistic educators	Values clarification, emotional literacy, collaborative learning, meta cognition, holism, caring, creativity, transformation, alternative pedagogies
1970s/1990s	Constructivist educators	
1980s/1990s	Constructive postmodernism	

Source: Extracted from Stack, quoted in the Holistic Education Network, 2004.

The Holistic Education Network (2011) sees holistic education as

(i) being concerned with the growth of every person's intellectual, emotional, social, physical, artistic, creative and spiritual potentials;
(ii) being a quest for understanding and meaning;
(iii) recognizing the innate potential of every student for intelligent, creative, systemic thinking;
(iv) recognizing that all knowledge is created within a cultural context and that the 'facts' are seldom more than shared points of view; and
(v) valuing spiritual literacy (in a non-sectarian sense) with spirituality being a state of connectedness to all life and honouring diversity in unity.

Nava (2000) integrated the ideas of holistic education and came up with six dimensions and their implications as captured in the Table 1. 2.

Table 1.2: Dimensions of Holistic Education

Dimension	*Literacy*	*Intelligence*
Cognitive: Thought processes, the capacity to reason logically.	Linguistic, Quantitative	Verbal/Linguistic logical/Mathematical
Social: All learning happens in a social context of shared meaning.	Social	Interpersonal
Emotional: All learning is accompanied by an emotional state which can greatly affect the learning outcome.	Emotional	Emotional
Corporal or Physical: All learning occurs in a physical body. Mind-body harmony is an important element in the quality of learning.	Physical	Body/Kinaesthetic Naturalistic
Aesthetic: Beauty is a key aspect of human existence. Artistic expression of inner life is key to a happy life.	Arts	Visual/Spatial Musical/Rhythmic
Spiritual: The total and direct experience of universal love that establishes a sense of compassion, fraternity and peace towards all beings.	Spiritual	Spiritual

Source: Nava's (2000). "Multidimensional Perspective: Integration in Holistic Education".

Osho (1997) elaborated about five dimensions of Holistic Education corresponding to different subjects in the school curriculum. It is described in his book 'The Greatest Challenge: Golden Future', which are displayed in Table 1.3 as below:

Table 1.3: Five Dimensions of Holistic Education Corresponding to School Subjects

Dimension	*Area of Curriculum*
Informative	Social Sciences, Languages
Sciences	Reality about physical world
Art of Living and a sense of humour	Training of transforming one's anger, hatred, jealousy into love and a language of laughter
Art and Creativity	Painting, Music, Pottery, Craftsmanship, Masonry (Skill Development)
Art of Dying and Art of Self Defence without weapons	All types of meditations, such as: Zen, Tao, Yoga, Hassidism, Martial Arts like Aikido, Jujitsu, Judo (self-defence cum meditation)

Therefore the philosophy of Holistic education refers to the idea that a system, a process or a field of study cannot be determined or explained by the sum of its component parts. Instead, the system as a whole would determine how its parts behave and if there is any deformity or drawback, then also an integrated approach would be workable as a whole. In simple term, holistic education is a process, which develops almost the seven aspects of human personality, such as: physical, mental, emotional, spiritual, vocational, environmental and social. These seven aspects are complete and competent in themselves; but when considered together, can produce an accomplished human being.

Purposes of Holistic Education

The purpose of holistic education is to prepare students to meet the challenges of life. It is very well said that life is education and education is life. Holistic education believes that it is important for young people to learn:

- about themselves
- about healthy relations and inter-relations
- societal values
- emotional maturity
- resilience

- to appreciate truth, beauty and goodness
- to comprehend difference between virtual and real world

Gone are the days, when our Indian system had prominence of extended family culture and joint family ties, which had really showered a healthy value system among our social network. During the times of globalization, urbanization and unhealthy race for material upliftment, it has squeezed the human competence to achieve 'target gains'. Schools, known as miniature forms of society, follow a stipulated, structured, assigned and prescribed curriculum to design the persons for the 'world of work', to give them the skill which may carry them to the ladder of material success by making them 'productive'.

The need of today's world is to create good human beings, who are not mere calculative and profit snatchers but carry empathy to produce a peaceful, liveable and happy society. We have already manufactured human machines, which have proved their success over other planets as well. Nevertheless, our society has almost lost the warmth in relationships, healthy value network, feeling of belongingness and true patriotism.

Need of Holistic Education

John Dewey remarked that education is not something to be forced upon children and youth from without; but it is the growth of capacity with which human beings are endowed at birth.

Radhakrishnan Commission (1948-49) has pointed out: "The fundamental principles of our Constitution call for spiritual training. How can we build values in human mind? Our attempt should be to suggest and persuade, not command or impose. The method of suggestion is by personal examples, daily life and works and books read from day-to-day".

A child is a centre of attraction for the school as well as parents. It is very well said that three persons have a great influence on the personality of a student—Guru, Teacher and Parents. The child born in an open society is exposed to an advanced technological world, where expectations of parents too are high from our education structure. Many a times they feel dissatisfied on the output of present formal education. Today children and adolescents have ample exposure to sophisticated technological gadgets and their minds are too much involved with 'push buttons and touch screens'. Unwanted use of computers, mobile phones, video games and their experience with virtual world has taken them far away from realities of the world and life. Somehow they have become emotionally week to face the difficult times in their actual lives. Suffering from various psycho-somatic problems, they tend to adopt various ways of destruction. Many of them cling to drugs; some go in hibernation; some just end their lives by committing suicide. This is really a sad state of affairs which is the major concern of the parents.

There are various factors responsible for this situation which is prevalent in our society and 'parenting' has become a real challenge in these days. The adolescents face a lot of pressure in the environment; such as

- increased competition in almost every field of their social life like sports, career, academics, co-curricular activities and other out-of-school chores.
- pressure about their self-image, looks, body shape with a dominant feeling "I should look smart and be appreciated by my peer group".
- negative impact of the environment; physical, visual, emotional, psychological, etc.
- social problems such as corruption, sense of insecurity, uncertainty of life, exploitation, physical abuse, etc. do have a negative impact on the growth of the young minds.

Over the last decade, research has demonstrated that emotional development, which is now termed as 'emotional literacy' is of fundamental importance. Learning emotional literacy has been shown to be crucial for intellectual development, social development, aesthetic development, and health. Studies have shown that resilience is not an inherent quality, but one that is learned. Resilience is fundamental to overcoming difficulties, facing challenges, and long-term success in any field. Children must learn resilience.

Plato has talked about higher and ultimate values, which are Truth, Beauty and Goodness. These values are directly related to different domains of person's physical and mental set up. This is explained in the following Table 1.4.

Table 1.4: Ultimate Values, their Relation and Implication

Value	*Domain of human mind*	*Implication*
Truth	Cognitive	Who am I? From where I have come? What is the purpose of my being here? Where shall I be after my death.
Beauty	Affective	What so ever is created by Almighty is JUST Beautiful.
Goodness	Cognitive	Doing good to other selflessly.

Our children need quality education which satisfies the core need of their domains. The intrinsic meaning of Beauty must be understood by them so that they don't waste their energy in the garb of temporary and unreal attractions. They must be prepared for a tough life through a 'reality check system'.

Human Personality: A Treasure Within

Human personality comprises of three aspects: Body, Mind and Soul. Rishi Patanjali, in 'Yoga Sutra' describes that every individual carries five sheaths (Panch Kosha) or layers of body; e.g. Annamaya Kosha (food), Pranamaya Kosha (Pranic energy), Manomaya Kosha (Mind), Vigyanmaya Kosha (Intellect or Wisdom) and Anandmaya Kosha (Blissful state). Socrates defined education to 'know thyself.' Jacques Delors (1996) in his paper titled 'Learning—The Treasure Within' elaborated certain potentialities and qualities present in every human being, which are physical strength, memory, aesthetic sense, imagination, reasoning power, aptitude to communicate, etc.

William Shakespeare very rightly remarked that we know what we are, but know not what we may be. Therefore, it is evident that hidden treasure of man's possibilities is of utmost importance and it is the basis of one's strength. 'Potential' speaks of the possibility of awakening something that is lying dormant and it is the task of a right education, which can exploit the potential to the fullest so that a new human being is created.

Adolescents are the rich potential for any nation's growth and development, provided they are educated in the right perspective. A misguided youth is worse than a nuclear bomb. Education holds the capacity to change the instinctive behaviour of an individual into a humane persona. A healthy value system is the panacea to develop a peaceful and secure society, in which every human being can exploit his potentialities to the maximum and further achieve immediate and ultimate aim of life. Adolescent of today, standing on the cross road while facing a dualistic value system, expects a functioning pedagogy to get right assistance for discriminating between right and wrong. It is the values, which form ideals of life, by which a man lives and makes furtherance of his life. Need of the hour is to train and educate our adolescents about sound value system in an industrious way, which may make them complete human beings, holding a strong character embedded with morality and ethics. The practice of a variety of methodologies with a missionary zeal by the teachers definitely brings a desirable change in the ideology of the adolescents. The bookish knowledge, not correlated with the practice, is a futile exercise even in the best framework of curriculum. Exertive and well-chosen strategies are required for reconstructing the aura of present society.

Scheme of Education

Demographically, India of today is at its youngest best. Nearly 65 per cent of Indian population is less than 35 years of age. Youth is a wonderful time period, which carries limitless energy and zeal to do something challenging. Youth is the future of the nation. Swami Vivekananda suggested the youth to practice virtue, for which he has put forward two principles of ancient Indian education: a) Truth is inherent in man, and b) Student has to practice and realize the knowledge of Brahman (ultimate) to achieve this aim. He further suggested the conditions necessary to be followed by the taught: purity and perseverance. He gave the philosophy of Vedanta to achieve the spirit of man-making and character building education. He invented that education must help people to build self-confidence and self-reliance, based on balanced human relationships. His emphasis was on physical health, culture of mind, power of concentration, self-control, tyaga and sacrifice through consistent practice of Yoga and Meditation. Vivekananda's method of teaching resembles to the heuristic method of the modern educationists. Jacques Delors elaborated four pillars of education, which correspond to the ideas of Swami Vivekanada. Delors recommended to base educational structure on four pillars: 'Learning to know, Learning to do, Learning to live together and Learning to be'.

Murthy (2003) reported that adolescents and youth adults in developing countries are experiencing high level of stress from various forces operating in school, home and fast expanding media. At the same time, there is a loss of protective functions of joint family and the community. It is important for the schools to provide life skills to all children as part of the educational experience. Life skills are living skills or abilities for adaptive and positive behaviour that enable individuals to deal effectively with demands and challenges of everyday life. Life skills education provides skills namely: critical and creative thinking, decision making, problem solving, interpersonal relationship, effective communication, coping with emotions, self-awareness and empathy, etc.

Role of a Teacher

Swami Vivekanand stated that the true teacher is he, who can immediately come down to the level of the student and transfer his soul to the student's soul and see through the student's eye and hear through his ears and understand through his mind. Such a teacher can really teach and none else. The duty of the teacher is to let his student grow on his own in a natural environment. He is to provide appropriate opportunities to unfold learners' capabilities and talent. As there is a close relationship between mind and body, both influence each other. Therefore, physical health and mental growth is to be taken care of simultaneously. Mind of students must be controlled and understood by the practice of meditation, concentration and ethical purity. He put three necessary conditions for the teacher who holds a significant responsibility to accomplish this challenging aim of education through formal environment. The teacher must know the spirit of the scripture, he must be a perfect human being, who is devoid of any selfish motive for money, but has a love for his mark in society. Viveka Sutra states, "Each soul is potentially divine. The goal is to manifest this divine within by controlling nature, external and internal. Do this either by work or worship or psychic control or philosophy—by one or more, or all of these three. This is the whole of religion. Doctrine or dogmas or rituals or books or temples or forms are but secondary details".

Emerson assigned a moral and ethical duty to the teacher and observed that a true teacher is one who awakens the learner from within. Swami Vivekananda rewarded a teacher with appreciable pronouns such as 'friend, philosopher and a guide'. Teachers are expected to instil the feeling of belongingness among learners by fostering collaboration rather than competition, togetherness rather than individualism. They need to focus on developing their students as a universal soul not a narrow creature who is self-centred and opportunistic.

Advocating the philosophy of Vedanta, Swami Vivekanand redirected Indian education system. He emphasised on three points necessary in education to make every man and every nation great. These are inculcating the virtue of goodness, absence of jealousy and suspicion, and helping those trying to be virtuous and doing good. The eight volumes of Swami Vivekanand's lectures, writings and letters are the reservoir of guidance, which radiate freshness of his unedited live speech. His dream of awakening Indian people for their material prosperity and spiritual growth reflect through his message of Vedanta, which is basically based on the ideals of liberation of modern India with awakened souls.

The recent declaration of June 21, as an International Day for Yoga is a milestone in Indian history, which may inspire Indian youth in particular and world youth in general, to achieve a balance between material prosperity and spiritual growth. It may further assist them to fulfil their ultimate aim of life: self realization.

Sri Aurobindo considered education insufficient without Yoga. In his view, the aim of education is primarily 'Integral Evolution', which is a two-fold process. It requires multi-dimensional growth and development on one hand and seeks a gradual progress towards higher level on the other. He states that education is a part of yoga; i.e. man's attempt to integral education. In other words, yoga is the culmination of education. Both education and yoga seek the same ultimate ideal of individual and social development; whereas educational practices exhaust their best means for this purpose, yoga takes up to lead man to perfection.

Hare (2010) stated that a programme of holistic education aims to encompass all aspects of personal learning and growth and emphasizes the development of active relationships at all levels, whether these are between the subject domains, between individuals and their peer groups and communities or between the individuals and the world around them. It is stated that without a holistic education, everyone is uneducated or rather educated in a dangerous way. The educated human being of today has learnt the language of individualism surrounded by hatred, jealousy, discontentment, unhealthy competition and illogic mind games afflicted with mental sickness. He has forgotten the language of laughter, love, sacrifice, forgiveness and sharing.

Lombardo (2008) developed a list of key academic virtues (with definitions, instructional material, and learning activities) related to students' personal and professional success. The list is as follows:

- The pursuit of excellence
- Self-responsibility and accountability
- Love of learning and knowledge—curiosity and wonder
- Love of thinking
- Truth, honesty, integrity, and authenticity
- Self-awareness and understanding
- Humility and open-mindedness
- Discipline and determination
- Justice and fairness
- Holism and balance
- Hope and optimism
- Mutual respect, social conscience and responsibility
- Courage
- Wisdom (the application of knowledge and ethics to life)

Holistic education is the need of the present era. The National Policy of Education (1986) and Programme of Action (1992) followed by National Curriculum Framework of School Education (1986, 2000) in India, reiterated the need for developing the personal and social qualities among learners. NCF-2005 has put emphasis on the implementation of the 'Continuous and Comprehensive Evaluation' (CCE) System. The Ministry of Human Resource Development has introduced this system in schools across the country, aiming at the holistic development of the learner. In this system, emphasis is given on the development of affective and psychomotor domains of learner's personality, such as: human values, attitudes, life-skills, physical and mental health. It is a noble idea to implement CCE, along with the enactment of the Right to Education Act, which aims to shift the focus from 'just academics' to 'holistic development' of the students and make them stress free. This new system includes the evaluation of scholastic and non-scholastic abilities of the students.

In accordance with the holistic system, students appear for six exams during one academic year, including four formative (FA) and two summative assessments (SA). In addition to that, students are to show their ability in various projects, assignments, activities and events, spread over the academic year. It is a combination of summative and formative assessments, which includes class tests, revision tests, oral tests, reading tests, social skills tests and so on. But other side of the coin is that in such a heavy traffic of tests, students get hardly 2-3 weeks off and then the new session starts. New date sheet for formative evaluation is handed over just after 2-3 weeks of the new session. The teachers and students make a struggle to cover the syllabus and performing other prescribed activities. Summer break is given with a huge 'holiday homework.' And it follows another FA and the show moves on.

The worst side of this practice is that this CCE System is five years old and it immediately requires a thorough review to find its achievements and failures, because it was implemented with an objective to reduce the workload and exam phobia. It has actually increased the workload and revolved all the focus around the exams throughout the session. It has reduced the teacher to a record keeper, because he is busy most of the times in recording the activities of his students rather teaching them. When the number of areas, on which the student is to be evaluated, is increased, there is no time, energy and scope left for a child-centred and interactive classroom teaching. Though the grade system has been introduced to remove the 'marks phobia' from the minds of students and made them stress free, the whole year's activities drag the system again into the whirlpool of tests and exams. Reality check concludes that only their nature and titles have been changed. It seems the CCE system inducts the students in twelve months' season of exams, as the word 'continuous' is suffixed in the abbreviation of CCE.

While observing the real problems in the practice of CCE, it appears that the idea of holistic development has been squeezed to 'a system of holes'. This implies that we are confronted with a particular type of education and evaluation system, which does not project what the promoters actually dreamt of. Short term semesters tagged with a variety of exams have confused the students and their parents. Overcrowded class rooms with misappropriate pupil-teacher ratio has left the teachers perplexed. Individual differences in the class is somehow neglected. Moreover, all the students are evaluated in routine on a five-point grading scale for co-scholastic achievements. Recently, it is reported that Central Board of Secondary Education (CBSE) may dissolve CCE, which was started in 2009. It has withdrawn its optional policy, making class 10th public exams mandatory from 2018.

Lombardo (2011) stated that the six goals decided upon by faculty were intended to be holistic and comprehensive, providing a solid foundation for any further studies:

- Communication skills (Including composition)
- Independent learning skills
- Information literacy and acquisition
- Higher order cognitive skills
- Interpersonal skills and social awareness
- Self-development

Therefore, holistic education needs a careful and comprehensive practical application, which may bring quality based outcomes. We can take direction from ancient Indian philosophies and education system, which were firmly based on rich and healthy values.

2

Yoga—An Overview

Remain in bliss in this world,
Fearless, pure in heart,
Wake up in bliss every morning,
Carry out all your duties in bliss,
Remain in bliss in weal and woe,
In criticism and insult,
Remain in bliss unaffected,
Remain in bliss, pardoning everybody.

—*Rabindranath Tagore*

All the orthodox systems of Indian Philosophy have one goal in view, the liberation of the soul through perfection. The method is by Yoga. —*Swami Vivekananda*

Swami Satyananda Saraswati in his book, 'Asana, Pranayama Mudra Bandha' comments:

> "Yoga is not an ancient myth buried in oblivion. It is the most valuable inheritance of the present. It is the essential need of today and the culture of tomorrow."

Maharshi Patanjali introduced a very fundamental and comprehensive treatise on yoga in Sanskrit called 'Yoga-Shastra'. Sage Patanjali's book on yoga is a collection of 196 *sutras,* which are clear, concise and accurate. He defined the essence of yoga in the first sutras as "yogah chitta vritti nirodah," which means "Yoga is restraint of mental operation (process)". In this sutra 'chitta' means mind; 'vritti' means mental operation; 'nirodah' means restraint.

Yoga-Shastra answers some of life's profound questions, such as "Who am I, why am I born, what is the purpose of my life, why this existence is created, who is the Creator, where I was before this birth, where shall I be after my death, How do I deal with my life and its problems and how can I be peaceful forever". Yoga provides answers to these questions and many more. It makes a person more inquisitive. It unites an individual with the inner self.

According to Maharshi Patanjali, a yogi is one who is not affected by the ups and downs in his life. He becomes a *sakshi*—observer, watchman, and witnesses all the fluctuations occuring at his physical and mental spheres. To reach this state, Patanjali advocates a perfectly organised path of practice called *Ashtanga yoga* i.e., eight fold path. In the words of yogi-seer Sriranga Sadguru,

> "The customs and habits, the dress and ornaments, the manners and etiquette, the conceptions of right and wrong and of good and evil, the learning, literature and the various arts like music, the political thoughts, views regarding all actions and the consecratory ceremonies, etc. of the Indians (Bharatiyas), are all permeated like the warp and woof by Ashtanga Yoga".

Yoga being a 5,000 year old Indian discipline, focusses on the overall (physical, mental and spiritual) aspects of human personality. The Upanishads, composed in the 8th or 9th century BC, as a collection of beautiful verses, crystallized deep philosophical ideas that had a timeless quality and a vision of life in which yoga was a fundamental factor. The *Katha Upanishad* of 3,000 years ago says:

> "He, whose senses are uncontrolled, who is not tranquil, whose mind is not at rest, can never attain the true self even through knowledge".

It further states: "The Supreme Being formless, cannot be discerned by the senses, hence all knowledge of the eternal must be acquainted by the more subtle faculties. These are developed only through the purifying practice of meditation".

Yoga basically aims to transform body and mind by bringing it into sound state. Yoga refers to union or communication. The spiritual seekers of ancient times have gathered this treasure of yoga through their consistent introspection and practice of meditation and *samadhi* in the caves of Himalayas. They could do it with their consistent and self-directed will power, without any physical support of modern scientific laboratories and instruments.

The present society is struggling with various problems like stress related diseases, breaking up of families, dissatisfied youth, student unrest, drug addiction by boys and girls, women exploitation, dualistic value system, mental and social problems and an imbalance between material prosperity and spiritual growth, etc. Taking an overview, it seems the society is deteriorating day by day. Today an individual is disconnected from his self, and runs from pillar to post in the search of happiness and peace. Even though, an individual enjoys success and achievement, he/she still hankers for more and more, with a long 'to do list'. This endless desire drives a person towards a shorter life span. Our spiritual masters and eminent educationists have blessed us with a treasure of wisdom to enable us to peep into our hidden potential. However, our endless desires deprive us of the wisdom to bring out the best in us.

Meaning of Yoga

According to Panini, the grammarian, the word "Yoga" is derived from two roots—*Vijur* and *Vuja*—one referring to yoking (*vijur yoga*) and the other to mental concentration (*yuj samadhan*) and to sense control (*Vij samjamane*). The principle theme of the Indian system of 'Yoga' is mental concentration. It also includes control of senses. Thus, the second derivation of the word 'yoga' consists in 'Citta vrittivirodhah', i.e. the silencing of (all) activities in the mind.

Shri Gadadhara, the teacher of logic (*Nyaya*) opined, "Re-Integration means identification (*samadhi*)". It is of two types, conscious and unconscious. Conscious identification is the state of full cognition, which means that in this state, the object of contemplation is actually witnessed and the mind is fixed upon it and this is characterized by the silencing of all thoughts, except that of the object contemplated upon. In unconscious identification, there remains nothing of the mind except the traces left by its previous activities. All intuitive perceptions come within the realm of unconscious identification.

According to Vendanta, yoga means 'supreme realization'. It is the re-union of the living self with the supreme self. The word 'Yoga' can also be used as an extension for knowledge, love, action, unity, oneness, wisdom, etc. Three aspects of mind—cognitive, connative and affective—direct it towards various activities such as attainment of knowledge (factual and false), imagination, the experience of being unconscious (deep sleep and dreamy stage) and conscious (memory). Gateway of knowledge are senses, direct experience, revelations, intuition, etc. Memory is the storehouse of all types of experiences which are designated as good and bad, corresponding to happiness and sadness. Human mind is a highly powerful reservoir of energy which can be a healthy comrade if directed appropriately, but can turn into a dangerous enemy if left untapped and unattended.

The Bhagvad Gita believes in the *karmayoga* (way of action). It explains that one should remain in action without worrying about its result or fruit. It should not be the fruit which motivates the man to act but his determination and dedication. It is this equanimity of mind, which is called Yoga.

According to the Puranas, yoga is the inclination of mind accompanied by an active desire to know about oneself. For example, 'Who Am I?'. Human behaviour is influenced by perception (different senses), and also instinct (love, jealousy, hunger, sex etc.). These energies if not channelized properly, can create havoc in an individual's life in particular and in the society in general. Yoga is a scientific and helpful technique to master the instinctive behaviour of human beings. The concept of 'libido' as explained by Freud, is the main force behind other impulses, passion, etc. Hatred, jealousy, love, repulsion, anger are the expressions of the impulses, emotions and feelings. Sometimes due to situational differences, the fulfilment of instincts/passion is not accomplished, leading to anxiety, stress, rage, irritability, which gets reflected adversely in the behaviour of an individual.

Lord Buddha talked of four noble truths. He perceived that the whole world is full of miseries which come from desire. He therefore recommended eight-fold path to get rid of this cycle of misery.

Attachment *(kama)* in yoga is considered as an inherent catalyst element responsible for determining human behaviour. All the thoughts are created in the mind; actions get directions from the thought/ideas emanating from the mind. Thus, yoga considers 'mind' as an important entity. It is the inclination of mind which enables a person to make right or wrong choices. Guru Nanak says that mind behaves like a pendulum, swinging towards body in one moment and towards spirit in the next moment. Less the knowledge of 'self', more the inclination towards worldly pleasures, and *vice versa.*

Yoga helps a person in releasing negative emotions or energy in the form of 'catharsis'. *Pranayama* and *asanas* are helpful for this purpose, which clean the material layer. The thought of positivity being generated while doing yoga changes the internal environment of the body. Yoga practised through body, breath and mind, can lead a person to detachment. It is also a process that results in complete cleaning and healing—of the self, by the self and through the self-leading to self realization.

Patanjali has defined the purpose of yoga as "Atha yoganushasanam", not "Atha Yogah shir vijnanam", nor "Atha Yoga samadhim". He has used the word 'anushasanam' for a definite reason. The word 'anushasanam' is translated as discipline, but not an imposed discipline. *Shasan* means 'to govern, to rule, to direct, to order, to organize, to discipline, to control'. 'Anu' is a prefix which means 'the subtle nature'. It is the subtle manifestation of human personality, nature, mind, behaviour, attitude, belief and life. This is undoubtedly a very broad, vast and also supreme definition of yoga.

Parmananda (1996) remarked that yogasanas and meditation help in creating harmony and feeling of oneness, improve concentration, and are also good stress busters.

Feuerstein (2002) advocated that yoga is like an ancient river with countless rapid eddies, loops, tributaries, and backwaters, extending over a vast, colourful terrain of many different habitats.

Yoga is the cessation of movement in the consciousness (Iyengar, 2004).

Kumar (2005) states that the science of yoga is a powerful stream of knowledge. Radiant physical health, serene mind, continuous spiritual uplift and ability for harmonious social living is experienced by yogic practitioners worldwide.

Thakur (2007) opined that Yoga is also *yogah chhittvirilli nirodhaha* (cessation of mental modification). It means that when we become disciplined, the disturbance in our nature goes away.

Yoga deals with practical aspect of our life and makes us aware and experience the higher dimensions of our nature or self. He also quoted the statement given by Swami Sivananda that 'an ounce of practice is more precious than tons of theory'.

History of Yoga

The history of yoga being approximately 5000 years old, has travelled a long journey starting from pre-vedic era and continues till date. Though it has faced endless ups and downs, it has survived all odds and is gaining momentum in the present era. Its footprints are found in the history books where Indus-Sarasvati civilization of the ancient world is discussed. Seals excavated from the Mohanjodaro site were found in yogic posture. They were sitting cross-legged with arms outstretched. The pose was of meditative state. Another seal showed a figure standing on its head, which is called *sheesh-asana* in yogic practices.

Feuerstein (2002) described complex socio-cultural process of India by organizing it into nine periods, expressing distinguishable cultural styles:

1. Pre Vedic Age (6500-4500 B.C.E.*
2. Vedic Age (4500-2500 B.C.E.)
3. Brahmanical Age (2500-1500 B.C.E.)
4. The Post-Vedic/Upanishadic Age (1500-1000 B.C.E.)
5. The Pre-classical Age or Epic Age (1000-100 B.C.E.)
6. The Classical Age (100 B.C.E. -500 C.E.*)
7. The Tantric/Puranic Age (500-1300 B.C.E.)
8. The Sectarian Age (1300-1700 A.D.*)
9. Modern Age (1700-Present)

Pre Vedic

Scholars believe that yoga grew out of Stone Age-Shamanism, because of the cultural similarities between modern Hinduism and Mehrgarh, a Neolithic settlement (now in Afghanistan). In fact, much of Hindu ideas, rituals and symbols of today appear to have

* B.C.E.: Before Common Era; C.E.: Common Era; and A.D.: Anno Domini.

their roots in this shamanistic culture of Mehrgarh. Early yoga and archaic shamanistic had much in common as both sought to transcend the human condition. The primary goal of shamanism was to heal members of the community and act as religious mediators. Archaic yoga was also community-oriented, as it attempted to discern the cosmic order through inner vision, and applied that order to daily living. Later, yoga evolved into a more inward experience, and yogis focused on their individual enlightenment and salvation.

Vedic

The Indus-Saraswati civilization also gave birth to the ancient text known as Vedas, the oldest scriptures in the world. The Vedas is a collection of hymns that praises a Higher power; it contains the oldest recorded yogic teachings and is considered divine revelation. Vedic yoga is characterized by ritualistic ceremonies, which requires yoga practitioners to transcend the limitations of the mind. David Frawley, a Vedic scholar writes, "Yoga can be traced back to the Rig Veda, itself the oldest Hindu text, which speaks about invoking the mind and insight to the Sun of Truth. Great teachers of early yoga include many famous Vedic sages like Vasishth, Yajanavalkya and Jaigishavya".

The earliest term for yoga was *tapas*. Literally, this ancient Sanskrit word means 'heat'. It is derived from the verbal root 'tap', meaning 'to burn' or to 'glow'. The term is often used in the Rigveda to describe the quality and work of the solar or the superficial fire. Yoga spiritualized the orientation of the earlier tradition of *tapas* by emphasizing self-transdence over the acquisition of magical powers. At the same time, the 'yogins' adopted and adapted many of the techniques and practices of the older tradition of *tapas*. Chastity remained central to its practice, as is clear from the eight-fold path outlined in the 'yoga-sutra' (Feuerstein, 2002)

Pre Classical Yoga

(i) Upanishadic

Sometime between 1800-1500 B.C., Gnostic text called the Upanishads appeared. The 200 or so scriptures comprising the

Upanishads explained the transcendental self (atman) and its relation to the ultimate reality (Brahman). The Karma doctrine is believed to have originated with the Upanishads as well. Just as the New Testament rests upon and furthers the Old Testament, so too, the Upanishads further expound upon the scriptures of the Vedas. The teachings of the Upanishads dawned the era of pre-classical yoga.

Around 1400 BC, a great sage named Vyasa, categorized the Vedic hymns in four Vedic texts we know today: Rig Veda (knowledge of Praise), Yajur Veda (knowledge of Sacrifice), Sama Veda (knowledge of Chants) and Atharva Veda (knowledge of Atharvan). In 1200 BC, the great enlightened teacher Rishabh started the tradition known as Jainism, which is also dedicated to the liberation of spirit. Then in 100 B.C., a second urbanization began along the banks of the Ganges river (the former Indus-Sarasvati civilization). Later, in the sixth century B.C., Lord Buddha spread the teachings of Buddhism, which stresses the importance of meditation and ethics over physical postures. Buddhism had some similarities with Hinduism. However, yoga sages saw the limitations of ignoring the physical purification process. Siddhartha Gautama, the first Buddhist, who was skilled in meditation, also studied and practised yoga and attained enlightenment.

Explicit examples of the concept and terminology of yoga appears in the Upanishadic text of the Vedanta, which is the culmination of all Vedic philosophy. In the Maitrayaniya Upanishad (ca* 200-300 BCE), yoga surfaces as:

"Shadanya-Yoga, the uniting discipline of the six limbs (*Shad-anga*), as expounded in Maitrayaniya-Upanishad: (1) breath control (*pranayama*), (2) sensory inhibition (*pratyahara*), (3) Meditation (*dhyana*), (4) concentration (*dharana*), (5) examination (*tarka*), and (6) ecstasy (*Samadhi*)".

The doctrine propounded in the 'Katha-Upanishad' is called 'adhyatma-yoga'—the yoga of deep self. Its target is the Supreme Being, which lies hidden in the "cave" of the human heart (Feuerstein, 2002). Of the 108 Upanishads of Muktika canon, 17 are considered yoga Upanishads.

---

* ca: approximately.

(ii) Bhagvad Gitâ

This ancient texts are the first scriptures devoted entirely to yoga. The Bhagwad Gita confirms that yoga was quite ancient by the time of its writing. Only 700 verses long, the Gita is a conversation between Prince Arjuna and Lord Krishna. Its primary message is to oppose evil in the world. The Gita earned its relevance because of its attempt to blend jnana-yoga, bhakti yoga, and karma-yoga together, unifying the various yogic traditions. Many schools during this era taught the way of reaching deep levels of meditation in order to surpass the mind and body system to achieve the true and limitless self. Lord Krishna taught yoga of wisdom (Jnâna-yoga) and yoga of action (karma-yoga).

Jaina yoga resembles its Hindu counterpart in its higher aspect. Jaina writers like Harichandra Suri have made use of some of the codifications of Patanjali. In his 'Yoga Bindu', he praises yoga by calling it 'wish filling tree'. Like Patanjali's yoga, the yoga of the Buddha comprises eight distinct members or "limbs" which is known as the 'noble eightfold path'. The first two members of the eightfold path are said to deal with understanding, the next three deal with behaviour and the last three with concentration. The first five can also be grouped under the heading 'socio-ethical' regulations, while the remaining three members are specifically yogic (Feuerstein, 2002).

Classical Yoga—Patanjali's Yoga Sutras

After the turn of the millennium, the spread of yoga in its different forms gave rise to the need for standardization. Thus, in the second century C.E., Patanjali composed a seminal text, 'Yoga-Sutras' and defined classical yoga. The 195 aphorisms or sutras that comprise the yoga-sutras, expound upon Raja-yoga (the eightfold yoga path). The yoga sutra is meant to be memorized as means of internalizing its wisdom. The eight limbs of classical yoga (Ashtang Yoga) are

(1) *Yama* or restraint,
(2) *Niyama,* or observance of purity, tolerance and study,,
(3) *Asana,* or physical postures/exercises,
(4) *Pranayama* or breath control,
(5) *Pratyahara,* or preparation for meditation,

(6) *Dharana*, or concentration,
(7) *Dhayana* or meditation, and
(8) *Samadhi* or absorption in the sublime.

Patanjali advocated the study of the sacred scriptures as part of the yogic practice, which became classical yoga's distinct feature.

Patanjali, whose own life is virtually unknown, had the impact of further spreading in compact form the essence of *Raja-Yoga*. Some legends speak of his being *Adinaga,* the first snake, the lower half of his body being that of a snake, upon which the great Hindu God Vishnu reclines. Many believe that he was the same Patanjali, who wrote commentaries on Panini's singular masterwork on Sanskrit grammar; others speak of the legends of his birth. A few even dispute his existence and attribute the yoga sutras to many authors, but this is highly unlikely due to the structural, linguistic and stylistic uniformity of the short work. His base is Hindu Samkhya philosophy; he was highly influenced by Upanishadas.

The real ground breaking characteristic of yoga-sutra, however, is its perception of philosophical dualism. Patanjali believed that separation of the matter (*prakriti*) and spirit (*purusha*) were necessary to cleanse the spirit to absolute purity. This is in stark contrast to pre-classical and vedic yoga, which adopts the unification of the body and the spirit. The teachings of Patanjali thus represent a departure from traditional non-dualistic yoga which laid the groundwork for post-classical yoga. For centuries, after Patanjali, the dualism of yoga was predominant. Yogis focused almost exclusively on meditation and neglected the *asanas*. They attempted to exit the mortal and merge with the ultimate reality through contemplation. But with the advent of alchemy, a precursor to chemistry, the yoga masters rekindled their belief in the body as a temple. Contemporary thought shifted to health, longevity and maintenance. As such, the yoga masters attempted to demonstrate that new yoga techniques fundamentally altered the body's biochemistry and made it immortal. This led to the pre-classical and vedic yogic belief about the primacy of the asanas and to the beginning of post-classical yoga.

Post Classical Yoga

The era of post-classical yoga gave rise to prolific literature, which included extensive writings on different branches of yoga like *Hatha* and the *Tantras*. There also came up several holistic schools for yoga. Post-classical yoga can best be defined as an appreciation of the present moment.

Hatha Yoga Pradipika

Hatha is a Sanskrit word meaning 'sun (ha)' and 'moon' (tha), representing opposing energies: hot and cold, male and female, positive and negative, similar but not completely analogous to *yin* and *yang*. The word 'ha' refers to the solar *nadi* (pingala) in the subtle body and 'tha' the lunar channel (*ida*). When the two components of the word are fixed together, 'hatha' becomes 'forceful', implying that powerful work must be done to purify the body. Yoga means to yoke or to join two things together, hence hatha yoga is meant to join together sun (masculine, active) energy with moon (feminine, receptive) energy, thus producing balance and greater power in an individual. The term 'Hatha Yoga' also has a more specific measuring to connote a special set of internal cleansing method, known as 'Shat Karmas' (Saraswati; 1987).

In the West, yoga is usually understood to refer to Hatha Yoga. Hatha Yoga is, however, a particular system propagated by Swami Swatamarama, a yogic sage of the 15th century in India. Hatha yoga, also known as the yoga of physical discipline (Feuerstein, 1990), is a form of Raja Yoga (Sivananda Yoga Vedanta Centre, 1996), which has recently become extremely popular in the West (Feuerstein, 1990; Corliss, 2001). The techniques of Hatha Yoga place particular emphasis on physical breathing and concentration methods for regulation of the body's energy (Iyengar, 2001). It is dedicated to Lord Adi Nath, another name of Lord Shiva who is considered the first guru to impart the secrets of Hatha Yoga to his divine consort Parvati.

Yoga in Modern Era

Modern yoga arrived in the United States during the late 1800's. It can be attributed to many gurus, including Swami Vivekananda, and their apostolic works. Vivekananda was a student of Ramakrishna, and he attended the Parliament of Religions in Chicago in 1893 and introduced yoga there. After being well accepted here; he later travelled all around the United States to spread the yoga tradition.

Most of the longer established postural yoga schools in United Kingdom (U.K.) have gone through similar developmental phases from the 1950's onwards. These are: Popularization (1950's to mid-1970), Consolidation (mid-1970's to late 1980's) and Acculturation (late 1980's to date). B.K.S. Iyengar established 'Iyengar Yoga' in Britain during 1954; the British Wheel of Yoga (known as BWY) got established in 1962. Since early 1990s, Pattabhi Jois' Astanga yoga has also gained popularity (Michelis, 2005).

Another yoga guru, who is perhaps the most popular, was Swami Paramhansa Yogananda, who founded the Self-Realization Fellowship. Yogananda wrote 'Autobiography of a Yogi' and his teachings enjoy immense popularity even today. Other yoga gurus include Krishnamurti and Maharishi Mahesh Yogi. Krishnamurti travelled widely, drawing large crowds and expounded upon Jnan-Yoga. It was Maharishi Mahesha Yogi, who popularized Transcendental Meditation (TM) in the 1960's.

Other most prominent yoga guru is Swami Sivananda, who served as a doctor in Malaysia and opened schools in America and Europe in 1960's and 1970's. Swami Sivananda's work is based on modified Five Principles of Yoga: (1) Proper relaxation (*savasna*) (2) Proper exercise (*asanas*) (3) Proper breathing (*pranayama*) (4) Proper diet (*vegetarian*), and (5) Positive thinking and meditation (*dhyana*). Swami Sivananda was declared the founder of the International Sivananda Yoga Vedanta Centres by his disciple Swami Vishnu Devananda, who had also written the 'Illustrated Book on Yoga'.

Swami Sivananda's other notable disciples include Swami Satchitananda, who introduced chanting and yoga to Woodstock; Swami Sivananda Radha, the woman who explored the connection between psychology and yoga; and Yogi Bhajan, who started teaching Kundalini Yoga in the 70's. He also founded the 3H organization (Healthy, Happy, Holy), which expanded its centres worldwide. There was also the great Sri Krishnamacharya, who taught Viniyoga Hatha Yoga. The Viniyoga tradition is continued by his son, Desikachar. Desikachar's brother-in- law, B.K.W. Iyenger also continued teaching Viniyoga Hatha yoga and had quite a large number of followers.

Other yoga masters including Sathya Sai Baba, had millions

of followers on the national and international map. Swami Satyananda, a follower of Bihar School of Yoga and Sri Sri Ravi Shankar of the 'Art of Living', both are working in India and abroad. Bhartiya Yog Sansthan, New Delhi, established in 1967 under the guidance of Shri Parkash Lal ji renders selfless service to the society in the field of yoga. 'Sahaja Yoga' was made popular by Shri Mata ji Nirmala Devi during 1970. Various schools have been established under the name 'Sahaja Yoga International Schools' where students learn 'Sahaja yoga' alongwith their general education. Swami Ramadev, the founder of Patanjali Yogpeeth, has brought a revolutionary awakening among people to realize the relevance of yoga in the modern stress prone times.

Joseph S. Alter, a scholar of Medical Anthropology from Princeton University, has elaborated on the changing form and significance of yoga in his book 'Yoga in Modern India' (2004).

> "Yoga's transformation into a popular activity idolized for its health value is based on modern ideas about science and medicine. The current interpretations of yoga and practitioners of yogic medicine and fitness combine the ideas of biology, physiology and anatomy with those of metaphysics."

Datta (2016) remarked that an explosion of scientific studies points towards yoga as a possible way to quality life in the future. From back pain to asthma, heart attack to blood pressure, depression to anti-ageing, sexual dysfunction to hypertension—yoga seems to hold the key that may open up a new scientific paradigm.

Types of Yoga

1. Hatha Yoga

According to the Monier Williams Sanskrit Dictionary, the word "hatha" means forceful. It is a strong practice done for purification. 'Hatha Yoga' follows the same principles as the 'Raja Yoga' of Patanjali, including 'yama' and 'niyama'. In the west, 'Hatha Yoga is mainly associated with the word 'yoga' and is practiced for getting the gains at the level of mental and physical health only, whereas traditional Hatha yoga is a holistic yogic path, which deals with human being as one single entity and a whole consisting of different phenomenon. This includes moral disciplines, physical exercises e.g. asanas (postures), pranayama (breath control), concentration, dharna, meditation (dhyana).

2. *Raja Yoga*

"It is said that the original propounder of classical yoga was Hiranyagarbha himself. It is Patanjali Maharishi, who formulated this science in to a definite system under the name of Ashtanga Yoga or Raja Yoga. This forms one of the *Shad-Darsananas* or Classical Systems of Philosophy. Vyasa has examined the original aphorisms or yoga sutras of Patanjali and this has been further elaborated through a class by a learned author named Vachaspati Mishra, and through the celebrated writings of Vijnana Bhikshu"—Sri Swami Sivananda. Raja yoga aims at controlling and checking thought waves. Whole sadhna is done with the mind. This yoga is also named as 'king of yogas'. It enables the individual to lead a disciplined and ethical life to have a sharp intellect, alert mind and full growth of personality.

The Brahma Kumaris World Spiritual University (BKWSU) was originated in Hyderabad (current-day Pakistan) during the 1930s. The university teaches to transcend labels associated with the body, such as race, nationality, religion, and gender, and endeavours to establish a global culture based 'soul-consciousness' as they call it. They follow the concept of Raja Yoga, where they view Yoga as a link established by single-minded, passionate, loveful and purposeful intellectual remembrance of God as it brings about the divinisation of man, i.e., purification of self, conquest of vices and attainment of sublime peace.

3. *Mantra Yoga or Japa Yoga*

Mantras (or mantarams) are words, phrases, or syllables which are chanted thoughtfully and with deep attention. The idea here is to make the mind aware and alert. Feelings are to be transcended. A constant practice of mantra chanting helps the individual to reveal super-conscious mind and experience a blissful state. The focused attention on the words and their meaning assists the wandering mind to stabilize and unfold its hidden potential. It further guides the mind to higher consciousness.

4. Bhakti Yoga

Bhakti yoga, or devotional yoga, is directly linked with our 'affective' domain of mind. The practitioner of this yoga is called 'bhakta' who visualizes, thinks, feels and realizes that his lord or God is in front of him and he talks to Him whom he considers his friend, parents, brother, king etc. The continuous and regular flow of selfless love carries the bhakta to the stage of super conscious, which is known as 'bhava'.

5. Karma Yoga

Attaining the oneness by selfless service to humanity without anticipating the result or any benefit, as Lord Krishna explains in Geeta:

> "Karmarne Vadhikaryasya Ma Phaleshu Kadhajewa"
> It means: 'Perform your duties without anticipating anything in return'.

Other yoga systems such as Kundalini yoga, Sivananda yoga, Integral yoga etc. are also prevalent in the society, which too are basically following a combination of yoga asanas, breathing exercises and meditation.

Every yoga system is following a pattern, which deals with three levels of an individual i.e. physical, mental and spiritual. Ashtanga yoga, Iyengar yoga, Hatha yoga, Raja yoga, Bikram yoga, Viniyoga etc. include Asanas, Pranayama, Meditation, Chanting, whereas Bhakti yoga and Mantra yoga focus on mental purification and spiritual upliftment. Karma yoga provides a philosophy, which educates the person about right actions to become a useful member of the society.

6. Iyengar Yoga

The Iyengar method of yoga is initially learnt through the in-depth study of asanas (physical posture) and pranayama (breath control). Shri BKS Iyenger has systematized over 200 classical yoga asanas and 14 different types of Pranayamas (with variations of many of them), from the simple to the incredible difficult. These have been structured and categorized so as to allow a beginner to progress surely and safely from basic posture to the most advanced as they gain flexibility, strength and sensitivity in mind, body and spirit.

Asanas and Pranayama are merely used as tools to master all eight aspects of Patanjali's Ashtanga yoga. The foundation of self-culture is to be built through practicing the first five disciplines of yoga. The experience of meditation comes when the student is ready. The prolonged practice of asana, pranayama and meditation affects the individual at the organic (physiological), mental and spiritual levels.

6. Bikram Yoga

It is also known as Hot Yoga. It is a style of yoga developed by Bikram Choudhury. Bikram yoga is ideally practiced in a room heated to 105° F (40.5^{O} C) with a humidity of 40 per cent. Classes are guided by specific dialogue, including 26 postures and two breathing exercises. Classes last approximately 90 minutes. This types of yoga is an effective tool for increasing flexibility because the heat helps tissues to stretch. But there are certain limitations of this practice. The people with cardio-vascular diseases can't perform Bikram yoga due to the strain placed on the body, when vigorously exercising in the heat. It may prove harmful for their health.

7. Viniyoga

This type of yoga includes asanas, pranayama, meditation and chanting. These are often a good form of yoga for those with back problems or neck injuries as they can be easily adapted.

8. Ashtang Yoga

Rishi Patanjali in his book 'Yogasutra' has written about Ashtanga Yoga. The word 'Ashtang' means eight-fold.

(i) *Yama:* These are the restraints and good commonsense guidelines to lead a peaceful and a healthier life. In Bhagwad Puranas, twelve yogic restraints are mentioned, whereas five yamas described in Patanjali's Yoga Sutra are the guidelines for how we interact with the outer world, the social disciplines to guide us in our relationship with others. They are called great universal vows or the *sarvabhauma maha vratas*, because they are not limited by either class, creed, time or circumstances. These five restraints are:

- *Ahimsa* (Nonviolence)
- *Satya* (Truthfulness)
- *Asteya* (Non-stealing)
- *Brahmcharya* (Celibacy, a behaviour which brings man nearer to divine)
- *Aparigraha* (Non-covetousness or Non-accumulation of worldly things)

(ii) *Niyamas:* These are the observances to be followed while interacting with one's internal world. Niyamas are about self-regulations, helping to maintain a congenial and positive environment to grow. According to sage Yajnavalkya, there are ten Niyamas and the Bhagvad Gita lists eleven constituents. Patanjali has given only five:

- *Shaucha* or Purity of mind and body,
- *Santosh* or contentment,
- *Tapa* or austerity,
- *Swadhyaya* or self-education (spiritual studies, recitation of Gayatri Mantra 'Om'), and
- *Ishwar*—Pranidhan or meditation on the Divine.

(iii) *Asana:* Aasana/yogasana is a posture in harmony with one's inner consciousness.

Functions: Functions of yogasana are basically five:

- Conative
- Cognitive
- Mental
- Intellectual
- Spiritual

Various Categories of Asanas:

- Standing Asanas—Tadasana, Trikonasana etc.
- Forward Bending Asanas—Paschimotanasana etc.
- Sitting and Supine Asanas—Padmasana, Vajrasana, Supta Badhakonasana,
- Inverted Asanas—suryanamaskar
- Abdominal and Lumbar Asanas—pawanmuktasana
- Twisting Asanas—Ardh Matsyendrasana

- Back bending Asanas—Bhujangasana, Ustrasana
- Balancing Asanas—Sarvangasana

(iv) *Pranayama:* Pranayama is the science of proper breathing. Breath is the main source of nourishment for all the cells of the body. The average person uses only about one-seventh of his total lung capacity. By learning how to increase this capacity with deep abdominal breathing, along with specific pranayama practices, we can increase the flow of vital energy to various organs in our body, and increase our immunity to various diseases and overcome many physical ailments. The way we breathe also has a profound effect on the nervous system. Our brain cells use three times more oxygen than other cells of the body. By regulating the breath and increasing oxygenation to brain cells, we help to strengthen and revitalize both the voluntary and automatic nervous system.

In the yogic point of view, if human beings wish to experience health or well-being, they have to approach their nature from different angles. They need to work at the same time with their body and their mind, with expressions of consciousness, which filter down into the mind and the body. The process of self-observation or self-understanding leads to the experience of optimal health and well-being. Thus, yoga is a method of realizing one's own potential for the purpose of healing.

More than a breath-control exercise, pranayama is all about controlling the life force or *prana*. Since *prana* or breath is the basis of life, the practice of paranayama helps in harnessing the prana in and around us, and by deepening and extending it, pranayama leads to a state of inner peace. According to Patanjali's yoga sutra, pranayama enables the mind to acquire the capacity to concentrate on any given object of attention.

"All that exists in all the three worlds is under the governance of Prana. Oh Prâna (please) protect us (your children) as mother and grant us the (real) wealth and wisdom".

This is the most comprehensive definition of Prâna found in Upanisadic and Yoga lore. Modern science has found that the basic fabric of the entire physical world is nothing, but energy. Prâna, in other words, is called life. This is in all beings. And Pranayama as defined in the Yoga Sutras of Patanjali is the science of cleansing, balancing and gaining control over the Prâna in the human system (Nagendra, 1999).

Forced unilateral nostril breathing modified EEG activity over the two hemispheres, with a greater amplitude on the side contra-lateral to the potent nostril. This was also believed to influence performance on specific tasks (Beubel, 1977; Klein *et al.*, 1986). Jella and Shannahoff Khalsa, (1993) showed that forced left nostril breathing increased spatial performance on a cognitive task.

Yogic practices were devised in ancient times to perhaps aid in realizing the capability of highest possible functional harmony in body and mind. Pranayamic exercises are among the important yogic practices (Vivekananda, 1973).

The ancient science of yoga makes use of voluntary regulation of the breathing to make respiration rhythmic, and to calm the mind. This practice is called Pranayama. Some varieties of Pranayama require the practitioner to inhale and exhale through one nostril selectively. These yogic practices provide an opportunity to study the effects of selective nostril breathing carried on effortlessly for prolonged periods. When each respiratory cycle is completed through the right nostril exclusively, the practice is called Surya Anuloma-Viloma Pranayama, which means "heat" generating breathing practice, and when completed through the left nostril alone, the practice is called Chandra Anuloma-Viloma Pranayama, which means a heat dissipating or cooling breathing practice. In Nadi Suddhi Pranayama (which means 'purification of subtle energy paths), inhalation and exhalation are through alternate nostril for successive respiratory cycles. These names were given based on the subjective experience of the ancient sages (Telles *et al.*, 1994). Yoga is an Indian science and way of life, which includes the practice of specific postures, regulated breathing and meditation (Tamini, 1961).

(*v*) *Praytyahara:* It involves rightly managing the senses and going beyond them instead of simply closing and suppressing them. It involves reining in the senses for increased attention rather than distraction. Pratyahara may be practiced with mantra meditation and visualization techniques.

(vi) *Dharana:* The last three limbs of Ashtanga yoga are the three essential stages of meditation to be followed step wise. Dharana involves developing and extending our powers of concentration. This consists of various ways of directing and controlling our attention and mind-fixing skills such as concentrating on the chakras or turning inwards.

(viii) *Dhyana:* In English language it is called Meditation. The word meditation is probably derived from the Latin word 'mederi' meaning 'to heal'. Meditation can certainly be a healing process, which cures the person emotionally, mentally as well as physically. Ultimate aim of meditation is to attain super-consciousness (wisdom) and peace of mind. It is the state of meditation, when the mind attains the ability to sustain its attention without getting distracted. Strictly speaking, unlike the other six limbs of yoga, this is not a technique but rather a state of mind, a delicate state of awareness. This state rightfully precedes the final state of Samadhi. Dhar (1996) viewed that there are many types of meditation aiming at the same destination, but through different pathways. Sources of all meditation in Veda or the source of eternal knowledge existed in the form of cosmic music since the creation of the universe.

A few types of meditation are mentioned below:

(a) *Yoga:* Sage Patanjali described eight steps to achieve the goal of super-consciousness (Udupa, 1983) through yoga described in Veda about 4000 years ago. One of eight steps is meditation. To start with meditation, first step is of one-pointedness, which is called 'Pratyahar'.

(b) *Vipasana:* Buddha, 2500 years ago, described vipasana meditation, in which a person sits in a comfortable posture with eyes closed and directs attention to the tip of his nose to observe his breath continuously. By this simple procedure, one learns to practice concentration of the mind. Gradually, one can make use of this method for meditation to attain peace and happiness (Dhar, 1997).

(c) *Transcendental Meditation (TM):* Maharishi Mahesh Yogi described a simple method popularly known as TM. The person assumes a comfortable sitting position with eyes closed and turns his attention inward to control his internal environment. Then he repeats certain sacred words called 'Mantra' for 20 minutes. Scientific evidences show that TM has definite effect on health in terms of reducing tension and all illnesses, improving intelligence and performance (Dhar, 1997)

(d) *Saral Meditation:* It is based on TM without mantra superimposed with consciousness to breath even when not doing meditation, when mind is free but without interfering with work (work is meditation) and other activities.

(e) *Others:* Promotion of mental health can also be obtained through Kundalini yoga (Gopi Krishna, 1975) and by using Zen Meditation as prescribed in Japan, Sufism as in the Middle East and Autogenic Training as in the Western countries (Udupa, 1983). Still recently, Gangchen (1995) has described five limitless meditations: i e immeasurable love, compassion, joy, equanimity and peace for achieving world peace.

Scientific evidence showed that yogic practices benefit in different disease conditions (Udupa, 1983; Dhar, 1997; Dhar, 1999). Vipasana meditation is 2500 years old, although its effect as a stress remedy made it popular only in recent years (Udupa, 1983; Dhar, 1997). Extensive studies have been reported on TM, which showed its effect on tension, reducing illness, improving intelligence and performance (Dhar 1997; Dhar, 1999). 'OM' meditation has been shown to cause mental alertness (Telles *et al.*, 1998).

Psychologists and yogic researchers of modern times too have found out what our ancient saints and scholars concluded about the various planes in which mind functions. These are: consciousness, unconsciousness, sub-consciousness and super-consciousness. It is a process of awareness which leads a person from one plane to the other. Prolonged practice of meditation helps him to achieve this state of super-consciousness.

Meditation is a mental exercise in which we direct our mind to think inwardly by shutting our sense organs to external stimulations. Meditation implies taking mind away from daily trivialities of life and focusing on something higher, something sacrosanct. It is controlling of our minds and thought processes. Meditation does not mean emptying the mind of thoughts, harnessing the mind to think positive thoughts. It is a vedic exercise, which can be used as a powerful instrument to restrain sense organs, control autonomic nervous system and also to attain super consciousness (Dhar, 1997; Udupa, 1983).

Mediation is concentration of the mind and relaxation of the body. The wavering nature of mind is highly dependent on the instability of the senses. To stabilize the mind, it has to be fixed on a single point to enable concentration. Normally, in meditation, this point is one's breath. As the mind gets fixed on one object, the concentration power increases (Mahaprajna, 2005).

Focusing the Mental Energy with Mantra

The word 'Mantra' is derived from the words 'manana' (thinking) and 'trana' (liberation). In other words, mantra is a potent form of thought, an instrument of conscious intention (Feuerstein, 2002).

Rama *et al.* (1976) remarked that mantra is an expression of a more evolved consciousness; it offers a unique link with that higher level. It not only makes the path to higher consciousness clearer by replacing interesting thoughts, its gradual incorporation pulls consciousness towards that state. Mantras are spandans, sound vibrations, which affect the different psychic centers of the body, the chakras. The mental repetition of mantra in a relaxed state of body and mind creates a set of vibrations within our multi-layered body. These vibrations create a force. Yogic mantras create a definite vibration in our psychic personality, mental and emotional personality, which helps to change the pattern. The original form of the mind is energy and the mind emits energy, which is subtle. When one begins to practice mantra, whether it is verbal or subtle really does not matter, because one creates different pattern of energy vibration in body as well as in mind. This creates energy pattern then acts like a magnet to attract the mental energies, which at present are being dissipated in all directions. It is the management of mental energy. The practice of pranayama is the most effective means to manage imbalances in the nervous system, the brain and the mind (Saraswati, 1995).

Modern science has now conclusively proved that the whole

of existence is just a vibration, a sound. In yoga, it is interpreted that the whole existence is just a sound. This is known as 'Nada Braham'. The entire creation is a complex amalgamation of sounds. Among this complex web of sounds, there are a few seconds, which are key sounds. These key sounds are referred to as Mantra (Vasudeva, 2005).

Brain Activity during Meditation

The brain is an electrochemical organ using electromagnetic energy to function. Electrical activity emanating from the brain is displayed in the form of brainwaves. There are four categories of these brainwaves. They range from the high amplitude, low frequency delta to low amplitude, high frequency beta. Men, women and children of all ages experience the same characteristics of brainwaves. They are consistent across cultures and country boundaries. During meditation, brain waves alter:

Beta: 13-30 cycles per second awaking awareness, extroversion, concentration, logical thinking, active conversation. A debater would be in high beta. A person making a speech, or a teacher teaching, or a talk show host, all would all be in beta when engaged in their work.

Alpha: 7-13 cycles per seconds—relaxation, non-arousal, meditation, hypnosis.

Theta: 4-7 cycles per seconds—day dreaming, dreaming, creativity, meditation, paranormal phenomena, out of body experiences, Extra sensory perception (ESP), shamanic journeys.

If a person driving on a freeway can't recall the last five miles, it is said that he/she is in a theta state, induced by the process of freeway driving. This can also occur in the shower or tub or even while shaving or brushing hair. It is a state where tasks become so automatic that a person can mentally disengage from them. The ideation that can take place during the theta state is often free flowing and occurs without censorship or guilt. It is typically a very positive mental state.

Delta: 1.5-4 cycles per second, deep dreamless sleep.

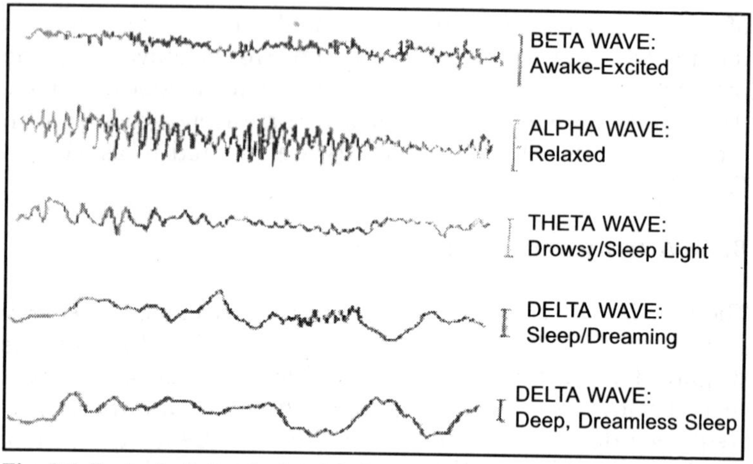

Fig. 2.1: Brain Activity during Meditation

According to the old scientific model in the West, the brain did not change much during a person's lifetime. The brain developed through stages such as childhood, adolescence and somewhere around age 20. But in 1980, a conference titled 'The Ever-changing Brain' presented scientific data to show that the brain is not a static "fixed-in-concrete" organ. New information corroborated strongly with what the ancient spiritual traditions of yoga said about the brain ability to change. The two important areas of the brain of particular interest to yogis (meditators) are the frontal lobes (in the area of the forehead right above the eyebrow), and the limbic system (deep inside the brain). The functions in the above two areas influence greatly the personality, thinking, attitude and behaviour of an individual. The limbic system is a primitive portion of the brain, present in both humans and lower animals, associated with survival instincts and basic primitive emotions such as rage, fear or aggression. Brain scans show that when people get very frightened, upset or angry, the cells in the limbic system start firing wildly. The frontal lobes located in the forehead, are the most anterior portion of the brain. The most important portion of this area is called pre-frontal lobes. They are the most evolved part of the human brain. Human happiness and ability to enjoy life is very much dependent on the function of our pre-frontal lobes. This area also seems to be associated with many of our best qualities such as idealism, joy, ability to concentrate, creativity and ability to think abstractly. Anything that makes us more restless or moody could decrease our pre-frontal lobe function and over stimulate our limbic system. There is a tremendous interaction between the limbic system and pre-frontal lobes. The basic interaction is that the pre-frontal lobes become stronger and the limbic system quieter. Meditation energizes the per-frontal lobes and, in time, the limbic system becomes harder to arouse. This results in behavioural changes, including better ego, integrity, fewer minor psychological problems, less depression and anxiety and better social skills. People tend to develop better anger management, more self-control and become more creative (Houten, 2003).

Samadhi: Samadhi or total absorption is the ability to become one with the true self and merge into the object of concentration. In this state of mind, the perceiver and the object of perception unite through the very act of perception—a true unity of all thought and action. This is the acme of all yogic endeavours—the ultimate yoga or connection between the individual and the universal soul.

Although, every step of Ashtang yoga carries with it a very significant role to bring a functional transformation in human personality, the three steps: Yogasanas, Pranayama and Dhyana (Trinity of Patanjali Yoga), when taken up as an integrated unit, become the base for a holistic development of the individual.

Physiological and Psychological Benefits of Meditation

Yoga is a wave sweeping the entire world today. Whether in the fields of physical fitness, medicine, psychology, sociology or philosophy, they are all benefiting immensely from yoga. It is practiced regularly today around the world.

Yoga is changing the way that we look at ourselves and other living beings in the world:"

In 2004, a review of eight studies on the effectiveness of yoga for the treatment of anxiety and other anxiety associated disorders was carried out. It found a number of encouraging results, which also included obsessive-compulsive disorder (Kirkwood *et al.*, 2005).

Yoga and meditation have been evaluated to be useful for children's development. Some of the school related benefits include anti-bullying, emotional balance, decreasing school behaviour referrals, increasing 'time on task' and improvement in academic performance by reducing stress. Yoga has also been found to be differentiated from exercise in improving health related outcome measures (Marie *et al.*, 2008; Ross & Thomas, 2010).

A review done by Innes & Vincent (2007) looked at 25 studies that evaluated the metabolic and clinical effects of yoga in adults with Diabetes Mellitus, type 2. Beneficial changes were found in several areas including glucose tolerance and insulin sensitivity, lipid profiles, blood pressure, oxidative stress, coagulation profiles, pulmonary function and specific clinical outcomes.

An Indian study of community home girls (in the age group of 12-16) used a matched pairs design and randomly allocated one of each pair to a daily programme of yoga games (Telles *et al.*, 1997). The community home girls were found to be initially higher than average children of the same age on the measures of physiological arousal. At the end of six months, heart rate and breath rate were measured, while children were sitting at ease for 15 minutes. Both the yoga and the games group showed a decrease in heart rate relative to initial values, while the yoga group also displayed a significant reduction in breath rate with breathing becoming more regular.

Another study of visually impaired children (age 11-17 years) indicated that participants in a three-week yoga programme exhibited a significant decrease in breathing rate (Telles and Sriniwas, 1998). Srivastava *et al.* (1999) found that yogic exercises are helpful in increasing chest expansion, height and grip strength and also in reducing the bulk in the body.

Yoga strengthens muscles and improves breathing techniques, and meditation releases stress and improves immunity (Vivo, 2013).

Yoga maintains good positive health of the body and mind. Selected routine of yogic exercises can certainly lead to a happy and successful life (Tripathi, 2005).

As far as the applications of yoga practices for management of mental problems are concerned, the yogic techniques are mostly being used as adjunct to the other psychosomatic rehabilitation and relaxation training. Many psychologists on the basis of their experimental results and clinical experiences found that yoga is an effective instrument of modification of human behaviour. Yoga more closely resembles the methods of psychotherapy, rather than a religion or a philosophy (Fritjof, 1981).

Yoga practices were found to be effective in the management of personality disorders (Singh, 1986; Tripathi, 1987), mental retardation, hyper kinetic behaviour (Subramanyam & Porkodi, 1981).

General Benefits of Yoga

There are various other general benefits of yoga as given below:

- Lowers Blood Pressure
- Lowers the levels of blood lactate, reducing anxiety attacks
- Decreases any stress related pain, such as headache, ulcer, insomnia, muscle and joint problems
- Increases serotonin production that improves mood and behaviour
- Improves immune system
- Increases the energy level
- Decreases anxiety, frustration, depression etc.
- Improves emotional stability
- Increases creativity
- Develops intuition
- Sharpens mind and intellect
- Increases self-awareness
- Relieves stress
- Helps in adjustment
- Increases positive energy
- Helpful to children with developmental disorders like Autism, ADHD etc.

The breathing techniques and specific asanas help in the improvement of concentration and make the child mentally healthy. Sun salutations and Kapal Bhati pranayama can help in losing weight. Regular practice of yoga provides inner peace.

3

Yoga and Holistic Development

The purpose of yoga is to create harmony in the physical, mental, psychological and spiritual aspects of the human being. Yoga is not mere a practice for an hour or two in the morning or evening, but it is a scientific way of living throughout day and night. It is to be merged as a habit. It is well said, "Yogasthah Kuru Karmani", which means, 'be established in yoga and do all your duties'. "Yogah Karmasu Kausaḷam" means that yoga is skill in action; it is in tune with the nature of Supreme Reality and Super Soul. Human mind, a wonderful gift of Almighty, consists of thoughts, emotions, desires, imaginations, inclinations, interests, feelings, reasoning etc. There are many hidden secrets of Creation which cannot be perceived by senses only. These dormant facts can be revealed only by deep contemplation by channelizing mental powers to the fullest. In the modern times, the whole world is passing through a phase of constant movement. High use of technology in all spheres (education, communication, transportation and so on...) has converted man in to a mere machine, completely at the mercy of technology.

Adolescence is the developmental phase that spans the transition period from the ending of relatively complete childhood reliance on parents to relatively independent management. Adolescence presents various problems for society, for families and for many adolescents as they make the obligatory passage between childhood to adulthood. Since the teen years are a time of semi dependence, they necessarily consist of a jarring mixture of freedom and constraints. In addition, considerable changes—physical, psycho-sexual, emotional, social—take place in adolescence (Dhavale *et al.*, 2002). In India, nearly one fifth of the population is of are adolescents. Materialistic attitude of the society has given birth to a mad race of competitions in every field of life. Too much expectations of the parents and school have led to a stressed living among the adolescent community. Their worth is just seen, counted and compared with their score card of academics. Today's adolescent student is suffering from many stress related diseases, such as depression, anxiety, insomnia, overeating, nervousness, fear phobia, headache etc. Examination fear, academic stress, role stress, vocational stress, social stress, family stress, self-concept stress, self-actualization stress, achievement stress, peer pressure etc., add an imbalance to his personality, and this load of stress instigates him to commit suicide or throws him in the world of drug addicts.

Factors like term writing, test anxiety, poor study skills, exercise academic load, profession and classroom environment are reported to be the causes of academic stress, which in turn forms a major part of general stress in adolescent students (Edmunds, 1984; Kagan and Squires, 1984. Archer and Lamin, 1985). An exploratory study of stressors and symptoms (Omizo *et al.*, 1988) revealed that stressors cited by intermediated and high school students are general adolescence problem, future and peer pressure. The school related problems, as specified by the participants are teacher's dislike, fear of failing, not doing homework, and failing to meet parental expectations.

Today's adolescent has become more aggressive, impatient and exposed to knowledge explosion, media expansion, and virtual world. He wants to have all glamour with the help of good income at a young age. His aspiration graph sometimes doesn't match with his input and the problem begins, which shatters him badly. He gets confused about the complexities of value system prevailing in the society and school. As adolescents are wealth of any nation, there is an urgent need to ponder over this serious menace. This has been well said by Dr. APJ Abdul Kalam, former President of India, in his book 'Ignited Minds' (2003):

> "I relied on the power and potential of youth. My young team never let me down. And what satisfaction there was in working with them on some of the most challenging situations. Given the freedom to achieve and guided properly, I am convinced the young of India can accomplish far more."

Various scholars have recommended Holistic Education as a solution to tackle adolescents' problems.

Lombardo, (2011) viewed the process of holistic education as that which covers the comprehensive content of the educational programme, highlighting the concepts of wisdom, heightened future consciousness, and ethical character development. This must further follow the characteristics given below:

- Future consciousness (personal and general)
- Personal and ethical character development
- Higher cognitive capacities (deep learning, critical thinking, creativity, and multiple modes of understanding)
- Communication, interpersonal skills and composition
- Historical consciousness
- Global and cultural consciousness and social conscience
- Ecological and environmental consciousness
- Science and technological awareness
- Information literacy and computer technology proficiency and awareness

As mentioned above, there is agreement among modern psychologists-cum-educationists, scientists and the great saints, and gurus of ancient India on an education system promoting the all round development of an individual. The ancient mystics recommended yoga almost 5000 years back. In modern times, researches on the effectiveness of yoga indicate that it has a variety of beneficial effects. A review of related literature has shown that yoga helps individuals to improve their physical, psychological and spiritual health.

"Yoga, as viewed by ancient Indian philosophers, has a direct bearing on the integrated development of the personality. Yoga, in its general methodology for the growth of man towards divine heights, includes techniques useful for therapeutic applications in making man healthier (Dora *et al.*, 2003). Regular practice of yoga builds up the personality at all levels, i.e. physical, mental, intellectual and emotional, in normal persons" (Udupa and Singh, 1972; Udupa *et al.*, 1973).

"Yogic practices were devised in ancient times to perhaps aid in realizing the capability of highest possible functional harmony in body and mind" (Vivekananda, 1973).

Domains of Human Personality and Yoga

There are seven domains of human personality:

1. Physical Health
2. Mental Well being
3. Intellectual Development
4. Social Adjustability
5. Emotional Maturity
6. Moral Upliftment
7. Spiritual Growth

Different domains of human personality are being discussed as follows. Research studies are also mentioned to show the impact of Yoga on these domains.

(i) Physical Health and Yoga

An ideal body has two main features:

(i) a proportionate body with all the muscles relaxed in normal state. It is soft like a flower, flexible to the core.
(ii) Instantaneously, it can acquire a diamond's hardness. All the organs and systems in the body with least abnormalities is the first feature of good personality at the physical level.

Second aspect of personality development at physical level is to make the body work more efficiently by using the energies in the most controlled fashion. At resting periods, all the muscles' metabolic rate is very low. During normal activities, just the necessary amount of energy is used by the body. At critical times, under conditions of high stress, the functions of the organs co-ordinate so nicely that the necessary amount of energy gets evoked and flows profusely into those regions, which need more energy. The body gets all the necessary strength to deal with the situation. This 'stamina' of harnessing of the inner vital energies and training the different organs and systems to work in such co-ordination can be effectively accomplished by yogic practices (Nagendra *et al.*, 1988).

In terms of general physical health, the accumulated evidence suggests that yoga practices are effective in the management of symptoms of wide range of diseases and disorders such as diabetes (Jain *et al.*, 1993), asthma (Nagarathana and Nagendra, 1985), hypertension (Patel, 1993) and Carpel tunnel syndrome (Garfinkel *et al.*, 1998). Current knowledge regarding the physiological effects of yoga in adults has also been summarized. Stabilization of the autonomic neurons system functions, improvement in endocrine system functions, improvement of thermoregulatory system, improved respiratory function and alpha wave activations were also found (Kimura *et al.*, 2002).

To date, most yoga research has been condition-specific, or relating to a particular life stage, or disorder, including, ageing, anxiety, ADHD (attention deficit/hyperactivity disorder), addiction, asthma, back pain, cardiovascular disease and fitness, carpal tunnel syndrome, childhood development, diabetes, depression (including post-natal depression), menopausal symptoms, multiple sclerosis, obsessive compulsive disorder, occupational health, osteoarthritis, seizure disorders, strength and flexibility, etc. As the benefits of yoga become more evident and widely known, further studies are being undertaken and yoga is being considered in the school curriculum as well.

(ii) Mental Well-being and Yoga

Mental health stands for the health of the mind. We have become conscious of the importance of bodily health, but only a small number of people realize that the health of mind is as important as that of body. A perfectly developed body is useless, unless it is directed by a well-balanced and capable mind (Mal, 1955).

According to Carter V. Good, in the Dictionary of Education (1958), the whole sameness of the mind analogous to the wholesomeness of body is implicit in physical health. Accordingly, mental health is concerned with the health of the mind and it functions in the same way as physical health is concerned with the health of the physical organs and their functioning.

Waltin (1951) defined mental health in a holistic way, not divided into compartments, leading to a balanced personality and normal behaviour. A person with good mental health is always consistent in his behaviour and does not have mood swings like honest on Sunday, dishonest on Monday, generous today, crabbed tomorrow, sometimes reasonable and logical and at other times confused and irrational.

J.A. Hadfield (1952) considered mental health as the full and harmonious functioning of the whole personality.

K.A. Menninger (1967) interpreted sound mental health as the adjustment of human beings to the world and to each other with maximum effectiveness and happiness. It is the ability to maintain even temper, an alert intelligence, socially considerate behaviour and a happy disposition.

WHO (2001) described mental health as a state of well-being in which the individuals realize their own abilities to cope with usual stresses of life, work productively and fruitfully, and also contribute to his or her community. The power of imagination (creativity) and steadfastness (will power) are the two main aspects of human mind which come under mental well-being.

Aurobindo categorizes mind according to its power—higher mind, illumined mind, intuitive mind, over mind and super mind.

Guru Nanak states that mind is a powerful agency and it possesses the potential to control and direct the total or partial functioning of human body.

The World Health Organization indicated that by the year 2020 childhood neuro-psychiatric disorders would rise internationally, proportionately by over 50 per cent, to become one of the five most common causes of morbidity, mortality and disability (Srivastava, 2007).

Dr. P.C. Shastri, President of the Indian Association for Child and Adolescent Mental Hospital (IACAM), Mumbai, stated that in the last 10 years, there has been almost a 400 per cent increase in mental health problems for children. A 2004 report in Lancet has stated that teenagers in Vellore in Tamilnadu had the highest suicide rate in the world. It is found that average suicide rate for males and females aged between 15-19 years in developing countries is about 4 and 70 respectively. The suicide rate for females in the above age group was 148 per 100,000 in UK (Srivastava, 2007). Experts agree that academic and learning related problems, anxiety, depression, aggression, stress and ADHD (Attention Deficit Hyperactivity Disorder), all need to be examined along with the mental health problem of children.

WHO (2011) gave an estimate that about 2.6 million young

people, aged 10 to 24 years, die each year and a much greater number of young people suffer from behavioural illnesses, which hinder their ability to grow and develop to their full potential. Nearly two-thirds of premature deaths and one-third of the total disease burden in adults are associated with conditions or behaviours initiated in their youth (*e.g.* tobacco use, physical inactivity, high risk sexual behaviours, injury and violence, etc.) At least 20 per cent of young people are likely to experience some form of mental illness, such as depression, mood disturbances, substance abuse, suicidal behaviours, eating disorders and many others. A meta-analysis of five psychiatric epidemiological studies done by Reddy & Chandrasekhar (1998) on Indian youth yielded an estimated prevalence of mental morbidity, including 16 mental and behavioural disorders (classified into eight groups of organic psychosis, schizophrenia, manic affective psychosis, manic depression, endogenous depression, mental retardation, epilepsy, phobia, generalized anxiety, neurotic depression, obsession and compulsion, hysteria, alcohol/drug addiction, somatisation, personality disorders and behavioural/emotional disorders) affecting 22.2 per 1000 in the age group of 15 to 24 years.

According to the World Health Organization (WHO) estimates, about one million people commit suicide each year. The National Crime Records Bureau (NCRB, 2012) reported that in India, nearly 1,36,000 persons voluntarily ended their lives in a suicidal act as per official reports in 2011. The official report indicates that age specific suicide rate among 15-29 years is on the rise, increasing from 3.73 to 3.96 per 1,00,000 population per year from 2002 to 2011.

Sahasi *et al.* (1989) found positive effect of yoga on anxiety. A relationship between the practice of yoga and benefits of mental health and overall wellness is apparent (Schaeffer, 2002). Jensen and Kenny (2004) studied the effect of yoga on the attention and behaviour of boys with attention deficit hyperactivity disorder (ADHD) and found improvement. Kirkwood *et al.* (2005) studied the effect of yoga on anxiety and anxiety disorders. They found encouraging results, particularly with obsessive compulsive disorders. Srivastava *et al.* (1999) found that yogic exercises are extremely helpful in increasing self-confidence. Tacon *et al.* (2003) revealed that mindfulness meditation reduced anxiety. Pilkington *et al.* (2005) reviewed systematically the research evidence on the effectiveness of yoga for depression. Researches were conducted between January and June 2004. Five randomized controlled trails were located, each of which utilized different forms of yoga interventions and in which, the severity of the condition ranged from mild to severe. All trails reported positive findings.

Khalsa (2004) reviewed the effects of yoga interventions on various components of mental and physical health, by primarily focusing on the evidence included in the review articles. Yoga has the potential to be implemented as a beneficial supportive/adjunct treatment that is relatively cost-effective. It can be practiced at least in part as a self-care behavioural treatment, providing life-long behavioural skill, enhancing self-efficacy and self-confidence. It is often associated with additional positive side effects.

(iii) Intellectual Development and Yoga

In the modern era of science, both sharp intellect and reason play a key role in the scheme of education. Rather than mechanical cramming up of information, thinking and understanding are valued more in the learning process. The children are taught right from the primary stage to think logically and scientifically. The capacity to analyse and correlate relevant information forms the functions of the intellect-concentration is the expression; precision is the outcome (Nagendra *et al.*, 1988).

Intellectual development includes:

- beginning to move from concrete (what is) to abstract thinking 'formal operations'.
- questioning and testing adults' statements, evaluating adults' values.
- Feeling acutely self-conscious, critical, idealistic, argumentative, self centered.
- Expanding interest, intense, short term enthusiasm.

Telles *et al.* (2000) studied the effect of yoga on cognition and found that after 30 days of yoga training, the trainees showed improved performance in maze tracing. Other meditation researches focusing on the effect of meditation on cognitive performance, have observed that when participants regularly meditated before studying or giving examinations, their academic scores improved (Fiebert and Mead, 1981; Hall, 1999). Another important body of research found that meditation improved attention regulation or concentration. Several other studies on meditators have determined that meditators scored significantly higher on the tests of attention than non-meditators (Rani and Rao, 2000; Redfering and Bowman, 1981). Foris (2005) analysed the effect of meditation on concentration. In this, the meditation group was to meditate once a day for 20 minutes for 6 weeks, while control group was asked to simply sit quietly for same period. It was found that meditators improved their concentration and also showed a significant improvement in their scores.

Tjoa (1972) and Tjoa (1975) found that 'Transcendental Meditation' programme increased intelligence of the school students. Miskiman (1972) revealed that Transcendental Meditation improved learning ability among university students. Collier (1973), Heaton *et al.* (1974) and Cory *et al.* (1974) revealed that academic performance improved due to Transcendental Meditation. Benson *et al.* (2000) studied the effect of relaxation response curriculum on middle school students, where they found an improvement in academic scores of the subjects. Uma *et al.* (1989) reported that yoga techniques loosened the joints and relaxed the musculature, and helped the students in improving their locomotor skills and basic controls. Yoga controls breathing, leading to increased psycho-motor co-ordination. It is a conscious process of winning control over the mind. As an effect of yogic practice, both the concentration and attention span improve, resulting in the increase of IQ and memory power.

(iv) Social Adjustability and Yoga

Adjustment is a state of life when the individual is more or less in harmony with personal, biological, social and psychological needs and the demands of the physical environment. The dictionary meaning of the word 'adjustment' is to make fit, make suitable, adapt, arrange, modify or harmonize. It is a state of mind in which a person feels that his/her needs have been or will be gratified. The satisfaction of needs must lie within the frame work and requirements of one's culture and society. If it happens, the individual remains adjusted to the environment, otherwise not (Mangal, 2009). Piaget studied the adjustment process from different angles. He used the term accommodation and assimilation to represent the alternation of oneself or environment as a means of adjustment. A person, who carries his values and standard of conduct without any change and maintains these in spite of major changes in social climate, is called assimilator. The man, who takes his standard from social context and changes his beliefs in accordance with the altered values of the society, is called accommodator (Chauhan, 2002).

The maturing and growing child develops not only in physical, mental and emotional behaviour, but also correspondingly in social development. The child's range of social activities is interwoven with other features of his growth like physical, mental and emotional. Language is the result of interrelation between mental and social behaviours. Jealousy, shyness, affection and sympathy are the result of interrelation between social and emotional forms of behaviour. In socialisation, three factors are included: (a) basic characteristics of protoplasm; (b) certain original mental equipment, i.e. cerebral cortex, and (c) certain effective and emotional development, which comprises ductless glands. In socialization, the changes pass from impatient, self-centred, pleasurable seeking infant, concerned only with himself and with his own survival to considering and caring for others. He attains education, learns self-control and eventually assumes some responsibility in the society (Kundu and Tutoo, 1988).

Brautigam (1972) reported increased adjustment (increased self-confidence, satisfaction and ability to handle one's situation) as an effect of Transcendental Meditation. Childs (1973) found improved interpersonal relationship, increased happiness and increased self-actualization as an effect of Transcendental Meditation.

Uma *et al.* (1989) reported that yogic practice include: (i) breathing exercise, pranayama (slow breathing techniques) and Kapalbhati (an act/process to cleanse the respiratory tract (10 minutes); (ii) Sithilikarana Vyayama (yoga exercises to loosen the joints) and Suryanamasakar (salutation to the sun by twelve count yoga postures—10 minutes); (iii) Yogasana—simple physical postures (standing, sitting, prone and supine positions with smooth, comfortable, bending movements and specific slow breathing procedures (the asana practices are performed with the subject maintaining the final posture with the body relaxed—

35 minutes), Savasana is performed last; and (iv) Meditation—5 minutes. All these were practiced for 5 hours a week for one year by 90 children with mental retardation of mild, moderate and severe degrees. It showed a significant improvement in social adaptation.

The practice of yoga is also known to reduce autonomic arousal (Wallace *et al.*, 1971; Joseph *et al.* (1981). Increased physical activity has been shown to reduce autonomic reactivity to mental stressors (Steptoe *et al.*, 1993). Aron *et al.* (1981) found that transcendental meditation increased sociability and social maturity. Eyerman (1981) reported that transcendental meditation showed an improvement in social behaviour of mentally retarded subjects.

(v) Emotional Maturity and Yoga

The word 'emotion' is derived from the latin word 'emotus', the participle to emovere, which means to move, or to be put in motion. The word 'emotion' is used in psychology to describe a state of excitement in the organism (Sandstrom, 1966).

- Emotion is an aroused state within an organism which may occur in response to internal stimuli or external stimuli (Lefton, 1985).
- Emotion is a response of whole organism involving physical arousal, expressive behaviour, conscious behaviour (Myres, 1995).
- Emotion is a complex affective experience that involves diffused physiological changes and can be expressed overtly in a characteristic behaviour pattern (Morris, 1979).
- Emotion is an affective experience that accompanies generalized linear adjustment and mental physiological stirred up states in an individual that shows itself in overt behaviour (Crow & Crow, 1973).

Yoga trains us to

(i) systematically sharpen and sensitize our emotions;
(ii) consciously expand and diffuse the overtones and such sanitization. An individual is not born with set patterns of emotional behaviour. The attitudes and feelings of an

> individual at any given moment have a profound effect upon the way he may react to any given situation. In emotional states, the entire body participates in the reactions that accompany the experience. Cross relationship and physical factors influence psychological growth and emotional factors influence physical growth (Kundu and Tutto, 1988). The physical environment or climate, food, rest, exercise, strain, fatigue and disease determine the rate and pattern of child's physical growth.

Thus, the emotional climate, love or lack of it, good or poor discipline, adequate or inadequate intelligence growth experiences, psychological strains or satisfaction, and other psychological factors will determine the rate and pattern of his intellectual and personality growth (Gabriel, 1969). Our emotions control our behaviours, especially at a crucial juncture. The challenges of the modern era pose a great threat to the emotional faculty of man, probably stronger than ever. Yet the culturing of the development of our emotional faculties finds no place in the whole scheme of education. Man looks lost amidst the atrocities of life, unable to overcome his emotional conflicts, blocks and turmoil. The result is deep unrest, agony and psycho-somatic ailments (Nagendra *et al.,* 1988).

Fehr *et al.* (1972) reported that the practice of Transcendental Meditation enhanced emotional maturity. Muktananda (1980) identified the extreme impact of meditation on the emotional balance of the mind. Meditation enhances detachment from mental formations in the mind and control of mind's engagement. BBC News (2000) reported that yoga helps students to keep their nerves cool and remain stress free. Tacon *et al.* (2003) found that mindfulness meditation helped to achieve emotional control. Valente and Marotta (2005) explored the impact of a regular practice of yoga in the personal and professional lives of psychotherapists. This impact was then categorized into common patterns that emerged as four themes addressing professional growth and the self-care of the therapists. These themes are: internal/self-awareness, emotional stability, acceptance of self and yoga as a way of life.

(vi) Moral Upliftment and Yoga

It means changes in the capacity to reason about the rightness or wrongness of various actions that occur with age (Baron, 2004), the changes in the ability to reason about what is right and what is wrong in a given situation (Carlo *et al.*, 1996, Carpendale and Krebs, 1995). Moral development is a field of psychology. Social psychologists such as Martin Hoffman and Jonathan Haidt base it on social and emotional developments that are a product of biology, such as empathy. Jean Piaget, Lawrence Kohlberg and Carol Gilligan have cognitive development approaches to moral development. To these theorists, morality forms in a series of constructive stages. Moral identity theorists, such as William Damon and Mordecai Nisan, see moral commitment as arising from the development of a self-identity that is defined by moral purposes. This moral self-identity leads to a sense of responsibility to pursue such purposes. Psycho-analysts such as Sigmund Freud believe that moral development is the product of aspects of the super-ego as guilt—shame avoidance (Wikipedia).

Moral upliftment includes:

- engaging in more complex decision making process.
- resolving moral dilemmas in terms of the expectations of others, i.e. family, friends or other significant persons or what the law or our society calls for in a given situation.

Kotchabhakdi *et al.* (1982) found that the practice of Transcendental Meditation improved moral judgement. Nidich (1975) revealed that outcome of transcendental meditation is greater moral maturity. Aron *et al.* (1981) and Nidich *et al.* (1986) concluded that Transcendental Meditation (TM) increased orientation towards positive values and greater moral maturity. Alexander, C., *et al.* (1991) reported that TM may foster maturation as measured by scales of ego, moral and cognitive development, intelligence, academic achievement, self-actualization and states of consciousness. Frequent meditators reported significantly fewer stressors and illness symptoms, lower levels of anxiety, hostility, depression and dysphoria and higher levels of positive affect and sensation seeking than did infrequent meditators (Beauchamp-Turner, *et al.* 1992).

(vii) Spiritual Growth and Yoga

A man may have a very sturdy physique, amazing creative power, a powerful intellect and a highly sensitized emotional grasp, yet may have no idea of spiritual progress. The person is on the march towards spirituality, when he moves towards the root of the intellect, the causal state of the mind and the substratum of emotions, when he starts looking inwards. After introspection, an inward look, an inner awareness, features the spiritual quest. In this state, the subtler layers of the mind unfold themselves and the inner dimensions of the personality open out (Nagendra *et al.*, 1988).

Meditation is the soul of spiritual life. Mental modifications are the root cause of all misery and their eradication is the science of yoga. Self awareness is the goal of yoga and the means is meditation (Siddhianathananda, 2001).

Thakur (2007) described that yoga deals with practical aspect of our life and makes us aware and experience the higher dimensions of our nature or self. Swami Sivananda has well said, "An ounce of practice is more precious than tons of theory". Kumar (2005) stated that the science of yoga is a powerful stream of knowledge. Radiant physical health, a serene mind, continuous spiritual upliftment and ability for harmonious social living is experienced by yogic practitioners worldwide. Rao (1995) described yoga as a system of psycho-therapy, which carries scientific and psychological significance and is helpful in attaining spiritual upliftment.

Yogi (1993) stated that transcendental meditation helps the individual to unfold his mind's potential for unlimited awareness, transcendental awareness, unity consciousness—a lively field of all potential, where every possibility is naturally available to the conscious mind. Krejci (1994) found that yoga helps the individual through its techniques of meditation to develop an attitude to live a life of lasting happiness and self-enjoyment. 'O' Connor and Anne Marie (2001) claimed that students find inner peace through 'Om' meditation.

Empirical data indicates that the Maharishi Effect is particularly evident; when pure consciousness is enlivened by large assemblies of individuals practicing Transcendental Meditation and TM Sidhi programme. Till date, over 40 studies, several of which have been published in top referred journals, have confirmed the Maharishi Effect as created by such large assemblies (Orme-Johnson, 1992).

Research studies have proved that yoga enables an individual to promote his holistic development. The resolution adopted by the UN General Assembly on December 11, 2014, "decides to proclaim 'June 21' as the International Day of Yoga". The resolution recognises that 'yoga provides a holistic approach to health and well-being' and that there should be 'wider dissemination of information about the benefits to the health of the world population'. Hon'ble Indian Prime Minister, Narendra Modi during his address to UN General Assembly on September 27, 2014 stated:

> "Yoga is an invaluable gift of India's ancient tradition. It embodies unity of mind and body; thought and action; restraint and fulfilment; harmony between man and nature; a holistic approach to health and well-being. It is not about exercise but to discover the sense of oneness with yourself, the world and the nature."

In suggesting June 21, which is the Summer Solstice, as the International Day of Yoga, Narendra Modi said, "It is the date which is the longest day of the year in the Northern Hemisphere and has special significance in many parts of the world."

Yogi and mystic, Sadhguru Jaggi Vasudeva notes the importance of this day in the yogic tradition: "On the day of the summer solstice, Adiyogi [the first yogi] turned south and first set his eyes on the Saptarishis or Seven Sages, who were his first disciples to carry the science of yoga to many parts of the world. It is wonderful that June 21 marks this momentous event in the history of humanity."

The description of Logo for International Day for Yoga is given as below:

- Folding of both hands in the logo Symbolise Yoga, the union, which reflects the union of Individual Consciousness with that of Universal Consciousness, a perfect harmony between mind and body, man and nature; a holistic approach to health and well-being.

- The brown leaves symbolise the Earth element, the green leaves symbolise the Nature, blue symbolises the Water element, brightness symbolises the Fire element and the Sun symbolise the source of energy and inspiration.
- The logo reflects harmony and peace for humanity, which is the essence of Yoga.

This is a historic step taken at international level to recognize yoga and its ultimate significance. There is a hope that Indian education system would rightly make use of yoga through holistic education for helping our young brigade to develop a deep awareness of themselves at the body, mind, intellect and spirit level.

4

Stress among Students and Yoga

An experimental research on the topic "Effectiveness of yoga in respect to stress and their relationship with academic performance at the secondary stage" was conducted by the author. Stress was studied as an independent variable whereas academic performance was taken up as a dependent variable. A value orientation programme, including a yoga module, was administrated as a treatment to the experimental group. As these variables play an enormous impact on students' development at academic, personal or social levels, we need to have an in depth understanding about them.

Concept of Stress

The concept of stress was introduced in Life Sciences by Hans Selye in 1936. Although some pioneering studies by Kahn Wolfe, Snock and Rosenthal (1964) and Kornhauser (1965) were undertaken in the early 1960's, and some other studies were done during the World War II period, this field of study gained momentum only in the second half of 1970's.

Stress was never an Indian concept. It is the product of globalisation and considered normal and a part of life. As stress has become a global phenomenon, a lot of research is being undertaken for the management of stress at national and international level. The problem lies in the acceptance of stress in the mind as a natural outcome. Thus stress is an indication of mismanagement at 'thought' level. The individual himself is responsible for creating a stressful situation. Scriptures rightly say that 'we become what we think'. Undoubtedly, a person is capable of making himself stress free by right thinking.

Meaning of Stress

Appley and Trumbull (1967) explained that psychological stress refers to effective behavioural and psychological responses to aversive stimuli.

Rees (1975) remarked that the term 'stress' is in fact Latin in origin, which was first used in the 15th century as shortened form of distress.

Warr and Wall (1975) defined stress in terms of an individual's experience of tension, anxiety, fear, discomfort and associated psychological disorders resulting from aspects of work situation, which depart from the optimum (either too little or too much work).

Selye (1976) defined stress as variation from one's state of being in 'Eustress', which is marked by a man, specific to any demand made on it to adapt.

Dunham (1976) defined stress as process of behavioural, emotional, mental and physical reactions caused by prolonged, increasing or new pressures, which are significantly greater than coping resources.

Kets de Vries (1979) had noted that each individual needs a moderate amount of stress to be alert and capable of functioning effectively. It may prove as an asset so long as it is tolerable and helps in creating healthy competition. It can also be stimulating, a valuable human response to challenge and change. While healthy tension improves performance by producing a challenge, excessive pressure can be distressing, leading to loss of effectiveness, and ultimately to ill health and breakdown.

Rao (1983) has very successfully traced the origin of stress in Indian thought. Going back to the Samkhya and Yoga Systems, he has pointed out that there were two Sanskrit words 'Klesa' and 'Dukha', which approximate stress. The Samkhya system postulates that the feeling of 'Dukha' or stress is experienced by the individual in the course of his/her interaction with the world around him/her. The system mentions three types of stress—Personal (*adhyatmik*), Situational (*adhibhok*) and Environmental (*adhidenik*). Personal stress can again be of two types, namely physiological and psychological (physical and mental).

Stress is our response to events that disrupts or threatens to disrupt our psychological functioning (Lazarus and Folkman, 1984; Taylor, 1999).

Whitman (1985) stated about the mechanism which explains why students perform badly under stress. He discussed about 'hyper vigilance' (excessive alertness to a stressful situation resulting in panic, for example, over studying for an exam) and 'premature closure' (quickly choosing a solution to end a stressful situation, for example, rushing through an exam).

Scott (1988) stated that stress is any unpleasant and disturbing emotional experience due to frustration.

Trend all (1989) interpreted stress as a multi-factorial concept, referring to the contribution of factors within the individual, the organization and in the society, which leads to the feeling of low self-worth or achievement or effectiveness, and coping within one's professional role.

Stratton and Hays (1991) defined stress as the effect on a person being subjected to noxious stimulation or the threat of such stimulation, particularly when he/she is unable to avoid or terminate the condition.

Stress is unique in the category of diseases. It has no biological carrier such as a germ or a virus. Rather it is the result of how our mind and body function and interact. It is psycho-somatic; the 'psyche' means 'mind' and 'soma' means 'body'. It is the consequence of how we regulate or don't regulate the mental and physical functioning of our being (Pestonjee, 1992).

Jarry and Jary (1995) advocated that stress is a state of tension produced by pressure or conflicting demands with which the person can't adequately cope.

Keenan (1998) observed that people tend to experience stress, when the pressures around them become excessive. The discomfort felt by them is termed as stress.

Atkinson (1999) observed stress as an attempt of demands over the individual's ability to meet them.

Hendrickson (2002) found various reasons for adolescents to experience stress, which include problems with peer, parents, larger family, school etc. It also includes problems like death of loved ones, shifting to a new home, injuries or severe illness, child abuse or sexual abuse, family or community violence, natural disaster and so on. He further mentions about signs of stress in adolescents such as withdrawal, anti-social behaviour, stealing, lying, aggression, rebellion at home, physical complaints, missing school or poor school performance, changes in eating and sleeping habits, loss of interest in activities that were previously enjoyed, difficulty in concentration, thoughts of death or suicide. He suggested relaxation techniques to tackle stress.

Baron (2004) remarked that stress is multi-faceted process that occurs as a reaction to events or situations in our environment (termed as stressors). Stress can, therefore, be best defined as a state of imbalance between demands made on people from outside sources and their capabilities to cope with them. An interesting feature of stress is the wide range of physical and psychological reactions felt differently by people experiencing a similar event or condition. Some may interpret the event as stressful, whereas others may simply take it in their stride. Moreover, a particular person may react quite differently to same stressor at different points in time.

The Indian Express (2007) reported that the findings of researchers of Rusk University Medical Centre of Chicago, US, stated that people who are often stressed out or depressed are far more likely to develop memory problems than those with sunnier dispositions.

Sharma (2007) reported that today's children are suffering from a new form of stress because of the changing scenario of society. The reasons for this new found stress among the children could be negative effects like conflict between parents leading to divorce or separation, abuse or neglect, poverty, school failures, illnesses, etc. Even positive events like moving to a new home, a new job for a parent, a new baby in the family, etc. generate stress in children. Striving for academic excellence and aspiring for professional colleges have led adolescents to a different kind of lifestyle, like late night study or waking up early for tuitions. Too much indulgence in non-physical activities like computer, mobile phone and television is also breeding high level of stress in them.

Stressors—The Activators of Stress

Although we normally think of stress as stemming from negative events in our lives, positive events such as getting married or receiving an unexpected job, promotion can also produce stress (Brown and Mc Gill, 1989).

Many events/situations which are stressful share several characteristics:

1. Being very intense, they produce a state of overload. It becomes difficult to adapt to them.
2. Evoke incompatible tendencies—to approach and to avoid some object or activity.
3. Become uncontrollable. Indeed, a great deal of evidence suggests that when people can produce, control or terminate an event or situation, they perceive it to be less stressful than when they feel less in control (Karasek and Therell, 1990; Rodin and Salovey, 1989)

Kindler and Ginsberg (1990) have explained the effects of too little and too high level of stress on performance. When there is little stress, performance is low. When the stress is too high, then also the performance could be low. Somewhere, between two extremes is the optimum level of stress, where one attains peak performance. This is graphically shown in the Figure 4.1 below:

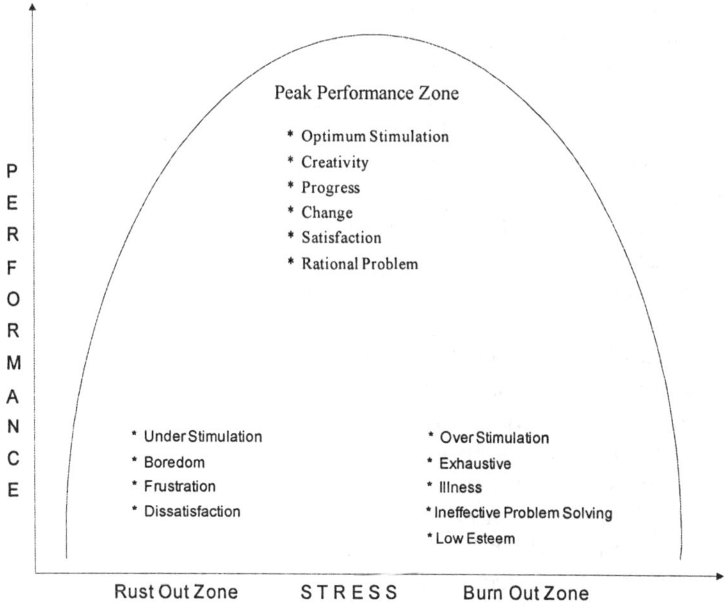

Sources: Kindler and Ginsberg (1990)

Fig. 4.1: Effect of Stress on Performance

Bhatia (2001) listed two types of causes of stress: (i) Family (parental pressure, constant comparison, nuclear families, both parents working), (ii) environment (competition, choosing the right option, media distraction, loss of value system, negative influence of western culture, constant comparison in school within peer, group).

Reactions of Stress

When a person is exposed to stressors, he generally experiences many physiological reactions such as high blood pressure, increased pulse rate and even sweating. These are part of a general pattern of reactions referred to as the fight-or-flight syndrome, a process controlled through the sympathetic nervous system.

Selye (1976) termed this sequence as the general adaptation syndrome (GAS), which consists of three stages: The first is the 'Alarm' stage in which the body prepares itself for immediate action. The arousal of the sympathetic nervous system releases hormones that help prepare the body to meet threats or dangers. If stress is prolonged, the 'resistance' stage begins. During this second stage, arousal is lower than during the alarm stage, but the body continues to draw on resources at an above-normal rate in order to cope effectively with the stressors. Continued exposure to the same stressor or additional stressors drains the body of its resources, and leads to the third stage 'Exhaustion'. During this stage, the capacity to resist is depleted, and the susceptibility to illnesses increases. In severe cases of prolonged physical stress, the result can be death.

Sailer *et al.* (1982) presented reactions of stress, which is given below in the Table 4.1.

Sarason *et al.* (2000) described some psychological, bodily and behavioural reactions of stress, which are shown in the Table 4.2.

A major group of disorder among Indian children are subscribed under the heading of externalizing and internalizing syndromes. (Achenbach and Edelbrock, 1978). These syndromes are displayed in the following Table 4.3:

Noshpitz and Coddington, (1990) have showed that people who have experienced multiple stresses in the recent past are especially susceptible to depression, anxiety and over-activity of physiological system.

Table 4.1: Reactions of Stress

Stressors	*Manifestations*
Subjective Reactions	Anxiety, depression and Low self-esteem.
Behavioural Reactions	Accident proneness, excessive eating, drinking, smoking, impulsive behaviour and drug abuse.
Cognitive Reactions	Inability to concentrate or make decision, frequent forgetfulness and hypersensitivity to criticism.
Physiological Reactions	Increased blood pressure and urine catecholamine and corticosteroids, increased blood glucose level, increased heart rate, and sweating, dizziness, headaches, ulcers and coronary heart diseases.

Table 4.2: Responses of Stress

Type	*Responses*
A Psychological	Feeling upset, inability to concentrate, irritability, loss of self-confidence, worry, difficulty in making decisions, racing thoughts, absent mindedness
B Bodily	Rapid pulse, pounding heart, increased perspiration, tensing of arm and leg muscles, shortness of breath, gritting of teeth
C Behavioural	Deterioration in performance effectiveness, smoking and use of alcohol or other recreational drugs, accident proneness, nervous mesmerism (foot tapping, nail biting), increased or decreased sleeping, increased or decreased eating

Table 4.3: External and Internal Syndromes

Externalizing Syndromes	*Internalizing Syndromes*
• Juvenile delinquency	• Depression
• Aggressiveness	• Withdrawal
• Temper tantrums	• Anxiety
• Lying	• Fears
• Stealing	• Obsessions
• Truancy	• Somatic complaints
• Impulsivity	• Schizoid features

Sarason *et al.* (2000) suggested relaxation training for the adolescents to tackle the problem of stress. It involves the following steps:

1. Focusing attention on a series of specific muscle groups

2. Tensing each group
3. Maintaining tension for five to seven seconds
4. Telling oneself to relax and immediately releasing tension
5. Focusing attention on each muscle group as it relaxes

A critical issue concerning stress among students is its effect on learning. The Yerkes-Dodson Law (1908) postulates that individuals under low and high stress learn the least and that those under moderate stress learn the most. A field study and laboratory tests support the notion that excessive stress is harmful to students' performance.

Akhtar (2006) reported following effects of stress:

- changes brain anatomy.
- Hippocampus, dealing with memory, shrinks forever.
- Stress module gets alerted. In the hypothalamus, neurons making the CRF or corticotrophin releasing factors are more in those, who have suffered severe stress. This CRF is part of a stress chain reaction. It triggers ACTH (adernocorticotropin hormone), which in turn sets off the adrenal gland to release stress hormones; adrenaline and cortisol.
- Effect of stress is not short lived in children having suffered trauma or abuse as infants. The changes in the brain anatomy are carried on to their adulthood.
- Changes are directly linked to body-mind problems, such as suicidal tendencies, severe depression, obsessive compulsive disorder, over reaction to simple stress or provocations, addictive behaviour, debilitating hypersensitivity that even affects immunity.
- Development of self-destructive behaviour.

The theory of stress and performance is based on the view that behaviour is a function of characteristics of the person and of the environment (Lewin, 1935; Murray, 1938)

Lazarus (1966) concluded that work anxiety and stress narrow the individual's focus and limits his ability to think creatively.

Research Studies and Surveys showing Students under Stress

The casualty graph of adolescents peaks sharply during

examination days and at the time of declaration of results. Their self-worth gets wrapped around academic performance. Academic stress and examination anxiety are cited as causal factors. Parents and children measure success in terms of material gains. It all began with the economy opening up and aggressive striving for financial gains.

Adolescence is an intriguing stage of development filled with many physical, cognitive, social and emotional changes. It has traditionally been viewed as beginning with the onset of puberty, a rapid spurt in physical growth accompanied by sexual maturation, and an ending when individuals assume the responsibilities associated with adult life—marriage, entry into work force and so on (Rice, 1992). Physical development takes place; facial features also undergo change during puberty (Berry, 1991, Berry and Mc Arthur, 1986). Cognitive development continues throughout adolescence (Klaczynski, 1977). Studies showed that adolescents experience huge swings in mood and turbulent outburst of emotions (Csikszentmihalyi and Larson, 1984). Friendship and social success also play an important role in social development of adolescents—the quest for a personal identity (Erikson, 1950, 1987).

Many teenagers find themselves in dysfunctional families—unable to meet children's needs which may harm them seriously (Amato, 1990, McKenry *et al.*, 1991). Some dysfunctional families neglect and even mistreat children. In some cases one or both parents being habitual drinkers or drug addicts, are unable to provide the kind of guidance, consistent control and support children need for successful development (Ge *et al.*, 1995). Research findings indicate that when these factors are lacking, children and adolescents are at increased risk, such as drug abuse, stealing, disobedience at home and at school, and overt aggression (Stice and Barrera, 1995). They may be subjected to sexual abuse, substance abuse, depression, withdrawal (shy), and may run away from home (Morrow and Sorell, 1989).

Suicidal thoughts and actions may be due to stresses and losses that the individual may not be able to cope with. Most of us harbour suicidal thoughts. Sigmund Freud called it the secret death wish. He believed that all human beings are born with 'Eros', the life instinct, which refers to joy, happiness, and 'Thantos', the death instinct, which refers to sadism, aggression and self-destruction.

Before Freud, Durkheim in his Manifesto of 1895 'Suicide', put forth the hypothesis that when social conditions fail to provide people with the necessary social goals at the appropriate levels of intensity, their socio-psychological health is impaired, and the most vulnerable among them commit suicide (Dhiman, 2002).

Adolescents are particularly vulnerable to committing suicide on account of emotional immaturity and temperamental instability. Parental expectations become largely incongruent with the children's ability, leading to frustration and depression. Students attempt suicide due to the feeling of worthlessness and the desire to escape social disapproval. Parents and teachers perpetuate the feeling of shame by scolding and beating. It can get worse when parents resort to subtler but worse methods like withdrawal of affection, inter-personal relationship, normal communication, etc. When there is no one to share the pain and anxiety, stress goes out of control (Grewal, 2003). Helplines run by NGOs in India revealed that maximum number of calls were received during the pre and post examination period. All the callers (teenagers) were on the urge of desperation, having no one to guide them (Agrawal, 2001).

In India, several studies have focused on the problem of mental health among children. These studies have revealed that morbidity is quite high in child population ranging 5per cent to 15per cent. Most of these children suffer from problems that are easily treatable-anxiety, hysteria, emotional and behavioural. These studies further revealed that the age group of 15-19 years is significantly the most vulnerable stage for developing mental disorder. It being an age of storm is likely to shatter the homeostasis of a growing individual (Basu, 1962; Chacko, 1969; Surya, 1964; Sethi, 1967; Dube, 1970; Srinivasamurthy, 1974; Rao, 1978, John, 1980; Jiloha, and Srinivasmurthy, 1983; Shariff, 1992 and ICMR, 1984).

Crow and Crow (1965) observed that the teenage period in human life is the greatest period of crisis and transition. During this period, several problems arise (Garrison, 1956). Adolescents are a problem to their parents, teachers and the society in general. They experience difficulty in adjusting to new roles at this stage and are therefore confused and anxious (Gardner, 1947).

A large body of research indicates that with increased stress, task performance may rise at first, but also fall within no time (Berlyne, 1967). Kets De Vries (1979) remarked that stress can be stimulating; it can be a valuable human response to challenge, as long as it is tolerable.

Offord *et al.* (1979) suggested an association between persistent scholastic problems and delinquent behaviour. Incidents of reported learning problems have ranged from one third to one half or even higher. John (1980) found that 21.43 per cent of children have some health problems like neurotic disorder, mixed environmental and conduct disorder. Adolescents' drug use has become a major social problem in America (Kandel, 1980; Weidman, 1983; MacDonald, 1984; Johnson *et al.*, 1985).

Researchers recorded that depiction of violence in movies and TV programmes have negative effects on children: they disrupt their moral balance, make them aggressive, affect their learning and thinking ability. They further discovered that aggression, academics, unpopularity with peer and violence are correlated among US children, which add to their frustration (Huesmann; 1985; Cheyney; 1983).

An ICMR (1984) study showed that totally 1853 children and adolescents were referred to child guidance clinics. Among them, boys were twice the number of girls. They had different problems like severe psychiatric disturbances, hysterical neurosis, conduct disorders, stammering and stuttering, psychogenic headache, adjustment problems and scholastic backwardness. When the symptoms were arranged in the decreasing order, school related problems occupied second position in the age group 6-11 years as well as 12-16 years in the total sample.

Jessor (1985) observed that early drug use was strongly associated with other problem behaviours such as lying, stealing, poor school performance and promiscuous sexual activity.

Mora de (1990) reported that the seventh and ninth grade students who interacted with peers with low academic self-concept were under stress and were viewed by teachers as experiencing academic problems.

Channabasavanna *et al.* (1990) studied 573 students (high school and above) and 407 non-students (young people) to understand the problem of school and substance abuse. The users of alcohol were 41.2per cent of the students and 33.75 per cent of non-students. As far as other substance abuse was concerned, the percentage were 11.9 for students and 7.5 for non-students.

David (1992) reported that suicide is the third leading cause of death among adolescents occurring at a rate of 10.8 per 1,00,000 among 15-19 years old. Suicide attempts were much more common occurring in 2 per cent of adolescent girls and 1 per cent of adolescent boys per year. Significant suicidal ideation (with the plan to commit suicide or intent to die) is more common occurring in 5-10 per cent children and adolescent youth. The study showed that depression is the single biggest risk factor, leading to suicide. The risk of suicide increases due to co-morbid anxiety, substance abuse or conduct disorder. Youth attempting suicide are impulsive and have poor problem-solving and social skills. Children with epilepsy have a higher suicide rate, which may be related to the side effect of the drug 'Phenobarbital'.

Fox (1993) found that certain studies have shown that anxiety effects performance negatively in tasks requiring attention abilities.

The Times of India (2007) reported that stress overloads our mental and physical resources and interferes the effective use of our skills, and adversely affects performance.

Cunha (1995) conducted a survey on academic stress among students and observed that they found studies boring. They did not like studying so many subjects. It was felt that too much academic pressure is placed on students and they are at a disadvantage of not being able to spend enough time for hobbies, sports and social get-togethers.

Philip and Kumari (1998) revealed that stress may lead to increased efforts in individuals sensitive to aversive stimuli.

Rao *et al.* (1998) observed that childhood and adolescence play a vital role in the development of personality. When genetic factors, parental attitude and rearing practices, sibling relationships, achievement in co-curricular activities, scholastic performance, school life, peer group, discipline procedures, school activities, social factors etc. are congenial and positive, the personality becomes happy and healthy. But when any factor either singly or in combination happens to be negative or deficit, a child or adolescent manifests some problem, disease, impairment, disability or handicap. Mostly children develop some psychological/psychiatric problems affecting their adjustment with others and performance in curricular and co-curricular activities.

Rao *et al.*, (1999) recommended that it is possible to achieve positive results through active collaboration of the school personnel and mental health professionals for the promotion of the well-being of students. For prevention of possible emotional disturbances, there should be early diagnosis and prompt intervention among them. It may be in the form of preventing certain mental health principles or learning about assertive behaviour or controlling irrational beliefs or practicing relaxation methods like yoga, meditation and prayers.

Gera and Ahuja (2001) studied the impact of classroom environment and academic stress of 9th graders. Scores on global achievement and scores on Maths, Science and English were analysed separately. They found that moderate classroom environment and low stress level yielded higher global achievement scores. Achievement of students in active moderate classroom environment was almost the same in English, Mathematics, Science, etc.

Mishra *et al.* (2002) in the study 'Adolescent Depression and Abuse' in two schools and colleges of Ahmedabad, India, involving 733 students reported that 37.5 per cent of the students scored positive for depression, sexual abuse 10per cent, physical abuse 6.3per cent, whereas 26.1per cent students reported emotional abuse.

Dhalve *et al.* (2002) conducted a study on junior college adolescents in Mumbai. In this study, a survey was conducted among 451 college students. It was found that 24.6per cent scored above the cut-off scores on the depression scale. A significantly higher prevalence of mental illness and substance use was also seen in the families of depressed sub group. 23.4per cent of the depressed group had abnormal eating habits and behaviour.

The Tribune (2002) quoted a report given by American Medical Association (AMA), which proved that drinking during adolescence leads to long-lasting brain damage, especially when it comes to learning, memory and critical thinking.

Verma *et al.* (2002) revealed that Indian middle-class adolescents face a highly competitive examination system. School work generated negative subjective states as reflected in low affect state, below-average activation levels, lower feeling of choice and higher social anxiety. The students, who spent more time doing homework, experienced lower average emotional states and more internalising problems, while those, who spent more time in leisure experienced more favourable states, but also reported higher academic anxiety and lower scholastic achievement.

A survey by the U.S. Medical Research Council (MRC) published in the Tribune (2003) found that stress levels in teenagers have reached a record high than what it was earlier. It has revealed that nearly one in four in the age group of 15 years, suffer from anxiety disorders, sleeplessness and forms of depression.

Sanyal (2003) reported that alcohol abuse among school children (14 years of age) is assuming very serious problem in India. Adolescents undergo manifold emotional and hormonal changes. Issues like career and higher studies are added to their stressful life, which carry them towards an easy resort i.e. alcohol.

Kouzma (2004) studied the main sources of stress reported by 423 Australian final year high school students using the academic stress questionnaire. As expected, the highest sources of stress were school related-examination and its outcome, anxiety over future, career choice, desire to earn, need to do well, etc

Zutshi (2005) reported that the stress graph of students reaches its peak during the examination days. Sometimes, students under continuous stress can take it no longer and fall into depression.

Gupta (2005), a psychiatrist for adolescents revealed that peer pressure, parents' pressure, academic pressure, high percentage achievement pressure are some of the factors which add to their stress.

Ahuja (2005) reported that due to easy access to soft drugs and peer pressure, a large section of students in Delhi took to smoking.

The Asian Age (2005) revealed new and important findings undertaken by British psychologists, who claim that tapping on a mobile phone or computer keypad or checking them for electronic messages temporarily knocks off upto 10 points of the users IQ. The rate of decline in intelligence compares unfavourably with the four-point drop in IQ associated with smoking marijuana. They have labelled the fleeting phenomenon of enhanced stupidity as 'info-mania', which means that they lose concentration as their minds remain fixed in an almost permanent state of readiness to react to technology instead of focusing on the task in hand. The brain also finds it hard to cope with juggling lots of task at once, reducing its overall effectiveness.

Parikh (2005) reported a survey conducted in New Delhi's schools under the 'School Mental Health Programme', which found that nearly 70 per cent students are suffering from stress and anxiety. Nearly one-third were reported having sleep disturbances, while one-sixth were using over the counter medication for headaches. The use of memory enhancing drugs is also on rise. 10 per cent had an increase in smoking habits. It further analysed that the anxiety level in those appearing for board exams are certainly high because of pressure from the parents. The competition level in schools is also increasing. The survey found that in 80 per cent of the cases, the reason for this anxiety was parental pressure. It listed other pressures on students:

- Academic pressure
- Peer pressure—students feel that if they do not score well, their friends would not accept them.
- Poor mental health
- Recognition and approval. This becomes very strong during board exams.

The survey suggested implementation of certain programmes, which would help the students to regain self-esteem, besides imparting skills to reduce stress.

IANS (2006) reported the suggestions given by prominent educationists to bring educational reforms in India. It stated that there is excessive domination by teachers in classrooms. Though parental pressure is growing, the Indian education system has been overwhelmed by the examination system. Aping British educational system in India has worsened the situation. The whole purpose of education is getting diluted, leading to more stress and suicide.

Jhingan (2006) reported the worry of NGO's, counsellors, psychiatrics, who claimed that hundreds of students continue to face stress and anxiety even after board exams. Parents' pressure really doubles the stress of the students. The Times of India (2007) reported that stress overloads our mental and physical resources and interferes with the effective use of our skills thus affects our performance badly. Bhatia (2008) reported the findings of the study conducted by the department of Psychiatry of the Government Medical College and Hospital, Chandigarh. The study titled 'Academics and Behavioural Problems in the Adolescent Population in Chandigarh' found that 25per cent of Chandigarh adolescent students suffer from psychological disorders. It further revealed that students are overburdened owing to high parental expectations, competitiveness and peer pressure.

Hindustan Times (2008) published the report of the Global Youth Tobacco Survey (GYTS) conducted in 140 countries, and India was one of them. Report says that more than one in five students, before the age of 15 use some form of tobacco in India. This survey was conducted with over 12,000 students between 13 and 15 years and threw up an alarming data which is displayed in the Table 4.4.

Another review of articles published in 1996, summarizes 21 studies on yoga in modern medicine (Bhala, 1996). This review one more time confirms: "Yoga therapy seems to be of great value in asthma, cardiac patients, multiple sclerosis, migraine, rheumatoid, arthritis and rehabilitation." These are conditions, in which stress may play a part in the course of the disease (Sapolsky, 1998). About 20 million children of ages 10-14 are estimated to be tobacco users according to a survey done by the National Sample Survey Organization of the Indian Government. To this astounding figure, about 5500 new users are added every day, making two million new users every year (Patel & Greydanes, 1999).

The Global Youth Tobacco Survey (Sinha *et al.*, 2006) showed that 4.2 per cent students of age group 13-15 years were smoking cigarettes and 13.6 per cent were using tobacco products other than cigarettes. A study done in Noida, Uttar Pradesh by Narain *et al.*, 2001 (Narain *et al.*, 2009) on students aged 11 to 19 years, found that tobacco use was found in 11.2 per cent students, 8.8 per cent were 'ever smokers' including current smokers, 4.6 per cent were 'ever tobacco chewers', including current chewers, 3.7 per cent were 'exclusive smokers' and 2.5 per cent were 'exclusive tobacco chewers'. The mean age of initiation of tobacco use was around 12.4 years. Nearly 70 per cent of boys and 80 per cent of girls = 15 years initiated the use of tobacco before the age of 11 year.

In college based study in Bangalore by Bhojani *et al.* (Bhojani, 2009), the prevalence of ever use of tobacco was 15.7 per cent, whereas 5.3 per cent were current tobacco users. Smoking was the predominant form of tobacco consumption among ever and current tobacco users. For 75 per cent of ever users of tobacco, the mean age for initiation of tobacco use was 14.7 (S.D. 2.05) years. Malhotra *et al.* in 2008 found that smokers constituted the single major 68

Table 4.4: Data of Global Youth Tobacco Survey

Puff prevalence	*Attitude*	*Availability*	*Advertising*	*Family and Friends*	*Trying to quit*	*Lesson learnt past*
14% currently use any tobacco product (Boys: 17.2%, Girls: 9.5%	32.2% think boys and 16.8% think girls, who smoke have more friends	9.6% usually smoke at home	74% saw anti-tobacco messages in the past month	26.5% live in homes where others smoke in their presence	70.6% want to stop, 55.5% tried to stop smoking in the past years	54.6% had been taught about the dangers of smoking. 37.2% had discussed in class reasons why people of their age smoke
12.2% had never smoked cigarette (Boys: 14.7% Girls: 8.9%)	30% think boys and 19.9% think girls, who smoke look more attractive	51.3% buy cigarettes.	71.6% saw pro-tobacco ads on billboards in the past month	40.2% are others who smoke outside home		35% have one or more parents who smoke
15.1% of those, who have never smoked are likely to start next year.		72.5% who bought cigarettes were not refused because of their age.	11.1% were offered free cigarettes by tobacco company representative			
		6.1% have most or all friends who smoke				

group (60%) of substance abusers, out of which 38 per cent were additionally using smokeless tobacco. Nicotine users reported peer-pressure as a single most important cause for initiation. Earlier studies have found alcohol to be one of the most prevalent substance of use in children and adolescent. A study shows that the age of first alcoholic beverage was 18.7 among male college students in Punjab, India (Khosla, *et al.*, 2008).

A study from NIMHANS on the Public Health Impact of Alcohol reported a reduction in the age of onset of drinking (Gururaj, 2006). Current studies however give conflicting results in the reporting of trends in alcohol dependence. A relative decrease in the percentage of subjects presenting with alcohol dependence has been reported (Basu, 2012 and Sachdev, *et al.*, 2002). These studies report a decrease in the percentage though there was an increase in the total number of patients dependent on alcohol. A study on Andaman school students by Sinha *et al.*,in 2006 showed onset of regular use of alcohol in late childhood, and early adolescence is associated with the highest rates of alcohol consumption in adult life as compared to later onset of drinking. Substance use among children and adolescents are on the rise and causes of serious concern (Murthy, 2010). Amongst the various substances, tobacco and alcohol use among adolescents have been studied the most. There is an alarming increase in the incidence of tobacco and alcohol use among young people. Abuse of volatile substances or inhalants has increased in children and adolescents due to its easy availability. Another trend which has been noted is the change in the type of opioids use, i.e. the increase in the number of prescription drugs being abused. Poly-substance abuse is also on the rise among young people (Agarwal *et al.*, 2013).

A population based cross-sectional study was conducted by Tsering *et al.* (2010), during June 2003 to May 2004 in two schools in West Bengal on 416 students. The overall prevalence rates among rural and urban students were 6.14 per cent and 0.6 per cent for illicit drug use, 8.60 per cent and 11.04 per cent for tobacco, and 7.37 per cent and 5.23 per cent for alcohol consumption, respectively. Both licit and illicit substance use was associated more with male students. This study also reported that the use of a substance by family members had a significant impact on its use by their children. The substance use was significantly high among male 65 students (45.8%) as compared to female students (7.3%).

Male students belonging to urban area were involved in substance abuse significantly more than the rural male students. The prevalence of substance use was found to be significantly more in the students who were living away from their homes.

In another study on substance use (tobacco, alcohol, cannabis, are canut/panmasala, opium, sedatives and hard drugs) among inter college students by Juyal *et al.* (2008), a total of 58.7 per cent students were found to be ever users, while 31.3 per cent were regular user of any substance. The prevalence of regular use of substances was significantly higher among urban students as compared to rural students (urban—37.9%, rural—24.4%). The abuse of substances was significantly more in male students as compared to 66 female students (45.8% and 7.3% respectively). Prevalence of substance abuse among various socio-economic classes was found to be highest in the middle class. Substance use was maximum among Hindus (32.0%), followed by Muslims (25.0%) and Sikhs (21.0%). A clinic based study by Malhotra *et al.* (2008) at the De-addiction and Treatment Centre of Postgraduate Institute of Medical Education and Research, Chandigarh between the periods 2002- 2006 on 173 subjects of age group 10-19 years, 83 per cent adolescents were in the 15-19 years age group, Hindu (80%), educated till High School (52%), single (94%), from nuclear family (69%) and from urban background (69%).

A study of substance use among higher secondary school students from Imphal, Manipur reported that the prevalence of tobacco and alcohol use was high among students. Familial use of substances was associated with the behaviour of adolescents. Friends were the key proximal determinant. The authors also recommended the introduction of a substance use prevention policy in schools to educate students about various adverse effects and to impart refusal skills (Ningombam, 2011). These studies suggest that substance abuse is fast becoming a public health problem among the children and adolescents of India. Tobacco and alcohol are the common substances of use. Substance abuse is commoner in males than in females. Family history of substance use is a common predisposing factor. In a study on substance abuse among school going male adolescents from Dehradun, 80.2 per cent of adolescent substance abusers expressed their desire to quit the habit (Saxena, 2010).

5

Yoga and Academic Performance

Another variable used in the research project was academic performance. The attributes of academic performance, such as concentration, memory and intelligence were studied.

Achievement is the proficiency of performance in a given skill or body of knowledge. It covers up all the fields, where learning takes place.

Meaning of Academic Achievement and Performance

Trow (1956) defines academic achievement as attained ability or degree of competence in school task, usually measured by standardized tests and expressed in grades or units based on norms derived from a vide sampling of pupil's performance.

Stephens (1956) states that academic achievement is the unique responsibility of all educational institutions to promote wholesome scholastic development of pupils alongwith other educational objectives.

Good (1959) is of the opinion that the status of pupil is recognised with respect to attained skill or knowledge as compared with other pupils or with schools adopted standard. Academic achievement is the one part of the wider term. It includes knowledge attained or skills developed in the school subjects that are usually evaluated by test scores or marks assigned by teachers or both. Thus, academic achievement is the knowledge and skills obtained by a student in various subjects taught at school. There seems to be considered similarities in as much as all of them place emphasis on knowledge attained or skills developed in the academic subjects usually designated by test scores. In other words, academic achievement refers to the degree or level of success or proficiency attained in some specific area concerning school or academic work.

Pressy *et al.* (1959) defined achievement as the 'Status or level of previous learning and the ability to apply what has been learned'. Achievement would not only include acquisition of knowledge and skills, but also attitudes and values as aspects of achievement.

Horrocks (1969) defined achievement as the status or level of person's skill, the range and depth of his knowledge or his proficiency in a designated area of learning or behaviour.

Crow and Crow (1969) defined achievement as an extent to which learner is profiting from instructions in a given area of learning. In other words, achievement is reflected by extent to which, a person from the training imparted to him has acquired the skill of knowledge. It is the outcome of general and specific learning experience.

Steinberger (1994) remarked that achievement encompasses student ability and performance. It is multidimensional. It is intricately related to human growth and cognitive, emotional, social and physical development; it reflects the whole child, it is not related to single instance, but occurs across time and levels through a student's life in school and working life. Thus achievement refers to the knowledge and skills gained from experience, an achieved level of expertise or performance in a specific domain.

Mehta (1969) expressed the view that the word performance is a wider term, which indicates both academic and co-curricular performance of the individual. Academic achievement refers to the degree or level of success attained in some specific area concerning scholastic or academic work. In general, it refers to the scores obtained in the annual examination. It has always been a vital factor in the life of an individual as it predicts future of the child.

Thus, there are various aspects of the concept of academic achievement, which has a great bearing on the personality of a student. From an early age, a sense of achievement is a source of good feeling and self-esteem, whereas failure a source of anger and self-reproach.

Thus, academic achievement may be defined as a measure of

knowledge, standing of skills in a specific subject or group of subjects. The academic achievement refers to achievement in a separate subject or total scores of several subjects combined. Hence, academic achievement is concerned with the quantity and quality of learning attained in a subject or group of subjects after a period of instructions. Academic achievement, therefore, signifies successfully carried out performance by an individual or a group as assessed after the completion of a task, whether it be academic, manual, personal, social or extra-curricular.

Various research studies are undertaken to see the effect of yoga and meditation on different mental processes of the subjects which affect their academic achievement.

Miskiman (1973) found that Transcendental Meditation (TM) improved problem solving ability of the students.

Shecter (1977) revealed that intellectual performance (increased problem solving ability) was increased due to use of TM by students in the classroom

Alexander *et al.* (1979) studied cognitive state development in children practicing the TM programme and found that achievement was improved.

Wallace *et al.* (1980) worked on the effect of TM programme on academic performance and revealed that academic performance increased due to TM programme.

Wallace *et al.* (1982) studied the effect of meditation in normal subjects and found that academic performance was improved.

Kember (1985) too found enhanced academic performance due to TM technique.

Warner (1986), Nidich *et al.* (1986), and Muehlman *et al.* (1988) found that academic achievement was increased when subjects practiced TM programme.

Jella and Shannah off-Khalsa (1993) studied the effect of forced left uni-nostril breathing on under graduate students, which showed increased spatial performance in cognitive task.

Benson *et al.* (2000) found improvement in academic performance after relaxation response curriculum. Sharma (2002) found that yoga can help to improve competitive performance. Shah *et al.* (2001) revealed that Saral Meditation improved the performance of the students.

Goldberg (2005) reported that by using latest high technology tools of neuroscience and bio-chemistry, the researchers of Mind/

Body Institute and the Harvard Medical School found positive and remarkable effects of Meditation on performance.

Motluk (2005) reported the findings of the research done by Bruce O'Hara and his colleagues at the University of Kentucky in Lexington, USA. These neuroscientists investigated the effect of meditation on brain functioning and found that each subject, who meditated showed an improvement in performance. Telles *et al.* (2006) found a significant effect of a one-month yoga training programme on the performance of a yoga group in a mirror-tracing task.

Attributes of Academic Performance

There are various variables which when join together influence academic achievement. Some of these are concentration, memory and intelligence which are considered as contributing variables.

(A) Concentration

Paying attention is a body function and therefore does not need to be taught. However paying attention as such is a function that is quite useless for the act of learning because it is only a fleeting occurrence. Attention usually shifts very quickly from one object or one thing to the next. The child must first be taught to focus his attention on a particular object for some length of time. When a person focuses his attention for a specific length of time, we call it concentration. Paying attention is a body function that makes the skill of concentration possible, just as the functions of seeing and hearing make the skills of looking and listening possible.

Concentration holds two pre-conditions: First, it is an act of will and cannot take place automatically. Second, it is also a skill, and therefore has to be taught.

Good (1945) stated that attention is the attributive state of sensory clearness, the active selection and emphasis of one component of a complex experience, a sensory adjustment of precluding for optical stimulation of a sense modality, adjustment of the sense organs to facilitate response to a particular stimulus or situation, and to inhabit response to extraneous stimulus or situation.

Sivananda (1974) defined concentration as a purely mental

process, not a muscular exercise. It is centering the mind on single thought. During concentration, the whole energy of the mind is collected, focused and concentrated on one idea or the object. The senses become still. There is no consciousness of the body and surroundings in deep concentration.

Concentration means wholeness, unity, equilibrium (Parmananda, 2000). Bhatnagar *et al.* (2001) described concentration as a focusing of attention (consciousness) upon a particular object. The process of concentration of attention has been accepted as a major factor in learning.

Swami Vivekananda enunciated 'Concentration and Detachment' as the principles of true education to achieve the goal of total development of an individual. This is what Patanjali portrayed in his second sutra while defining yoga.

"Yogah Citta Vritti Nirodhah"

It means Yoga is total control over mental modifications.

The capacity to concentrate helps to overcome the randomness of the mind. It is a skill to vanquish all thoughts totally and remain silent, giving way to the two fold process of mastery or control over the mind. Thus, the fundamental part of education is to achieve this mastery. What we are at, mostly in our education, is the former and not the later; it is a skill to calm down the mind as beautifully portrayed in the great text on yoga—Yogavashishta:

"Manah Prashamanopayah Yoga Ityabhidheeyate"

This aspect of relaxation and detachment is the missing part in our educational process. And that is the new dimension to be added in to our curriculum (Nagendra et al., 1988).

Concentration is the sixth distinct step of the Ashtang Yoga in Patanjali's Yoga Sutra, where concentration is defined as the attention of the mind stuff, which is directed in a single stream to a chosen field without being distracted.

(B) Memory

We cannot imagine life without memory. The very act of speaking means that we are remembering and recalling the words of our language in a grammatical sequence and we must keep track of what we have just said otherwise our conversation will be senseless. Memory of some sort is fundamental to our understanding of behaviour and mind.

If we trace history, we may say that interest in the field of memory was availed even in the medieval philosophers. Plato (427-347 B.C.) described the mind as a block of wax into which sensory experiences can be imprinted. However, the credit for the first systematic experimental study of memory goes to Ebbinghaus, (1885) who devised 23,000 nonsense syllables as a unit of memory. Experimenting on himself, Ebbinghaus memorized and then recalled hundreds of nonsense syllables as meaningless combinations of letters such as TEQ or PXT. He developed a systematic procedure for measuring memory. He was the first to plot a forgetting curve, showing the rate at which humans are able to retain lists of nonsense syllables after various interval of time. He found that at first, we forget materials we have memorized quite rapidly. Later, forgetting proceeds more slowly. Before him, it was thought that the effects of higher mental processes can only be observed and not measured.

Alexander (1953) has stated, that memory like learning is a fundamental process of adjustment. One of the most cardinal factors of adequate adjustment is the ability to profit by the past experience and it is obvious that, in the absence of memory, this ability would be impossible. There is no phase of human living untouched by memory.

Ryburn (1956) stated that the power that we have to 'store' our experiences, and to bring them into the field of our consciousness sometime after the experiences have occurred is termed memory.

Drever (1958) explained that memory is the experience of living organisms, in virtue of which what they experience leaves behind affects which modify the experience as a behaviour, in virtue of which they have a history and that history is recorded in themselves.

Woodworth (1970) defined that memory is the direct use of what is learnt.

Cognition refers to the processes through which, information coming from the senses is 'transformed, reduced, elaborated, recovered and used' (Neisser, 1976).

Lefton (1985) defined memory as the ability to recall or

remember past events or previously learnt information or skills.

The term 'information' refers simply to sensory input from the environment that informs us about something that is happening there. Cognitive processes are thus the mental processes involved in knowing about the world, as such they are important in perception, attention, thinking, problem solving and memory. The branch of psychology that deals with cognitive process is known as cognitive psychology, and the modern-day study of memory, since it emphasizes the mental processes involved in storing information and retrieving it from memory, is a point of cognitive psychology (Morgan *et al.*, 1986).

Bootzin (1991) stated that memory is the cognitive process of preserving current information for later use.

Crooks and Stein (1991) viewed that the term memory has a dual meaning. It refers to the process or processes whereby we store and preserve newly acquired information for later recall.

Bhatnagar and Saxena (2001) explained the process of memory that when an object is perceived, an image of it is imprinted in the mind or we can say that an Engram of object is constructed in the mind. It can be said that the mental process, by means of which we take advantage of a past experience is called memory. On the subject of memory, some psychologists have opined that it is not based upon Engrams, instead, aptitude and motivation make an important contribution to the development of memory. In fact, memory is a psycho-physical process, which is performed by the combined efforts of the mind as well as the body. It should also be known that whatever, we learn, we never remember forever. Maximum part of the learned material goes into conscious mind. When we need, we try to get that material into our conscious. Thus, memory is a process to bring our experience learned earlier, into our present.

Jain (2003) stated that memory is one of the important cognitive functions of human beings. Human beings have a unique feature of storing their experience. Thus, every experience leaves an impression on the mind and the memory deals with the reproduction of events and experiences of the past. Often, a person is aware of the memory when it fails, when for one reason or another, he/she simply cannot remember something. During such times, it becomes clear how much we depend on 'memory'. In common words, we can say that memory means remembering a particular event or experience. It may be defined as the reproduction of past events without the presence of actual stimulus. The act of memory consists of retaining and recalling the impressions. Retention is inactive and remembering is active, both are covered under general heading of memory.

Baron (2004) found that memory is the capacity to retain and later retrieve information. This definition is based on the basic model of human memory, which suggests that we actually possess three distinct memory systems:

1. Entering information into storage.
2. Retaining such input into varying periods of time.
3. Retrieving it when it is needed.

Webster's new world medical dictionary (2008) defines Short Term Memory as a system for temporarily storing and managing information required to carry out complex cognitive tasks such as learning, reasoning and comprehension.

The Information Processing Model of Memory (An overview)

There are a number of other theories of memory also, but the most common are the information processing explanation (Ashcraft, 2002; Hunt and Ellis 1999; Sternberg, 1999)

Early information processing views of memory used computer as a model. Like the computer, the human mind takes in information, performs operations on it to change its form and content, stores the information, retrieves it when needed and generates responses to it. Thus, processing involves gathering information and organising in the relation to what you already know or encoding; holding information or storage; and getting at the information when needed or retrieval. The whole system is guided by control processes that determine how and when information will flow through the system.

Figure 5.1 is a schematic representation of a typical information processing model of memory, derived from the ideas of several theorists (Atkinson and Shiffrin, 1968; Neisser, 1976; Gagne, 1985)

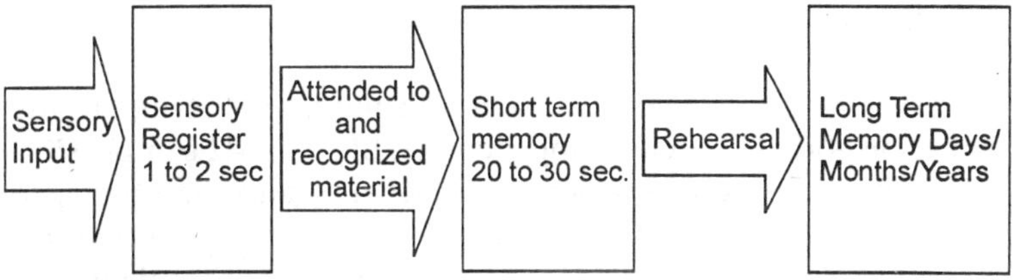

Fig. 5.1: The Schematic Representation of Information

Processing Model of Memory

The model consists of Sensory input, Attention, Short term memory and Long term memory, which are explained below:

Sensory Memory

Stimuli from our environment (sights, sounds, smell etc.) constantly bombard body's mechanism for seeing, hearing, tasting, smelling and feeling. Sensory memory is the initial processing that transforms these incoming stimuli into information so we can make sense of them. Even though sights and sounds may last only fractions of second, the transformations (information) that represent these sensations are briefly held in the sensory register or sensory information store so that this initial processing can take place (Bruning *et al.*, 1999).

The capacity of sensory memory is very large, and can take more information than we can possibly handle at once. But this vast amount of sensory information is fragile in duration. It lasts between one and three seconds. The sensory register holds information about the stimuli very briefly after the actual stimulus has left (Lindsay and Norman, 1977).

The information content of sensory memory resembles the sensations from the original stimulus. Visual sensations are coded briefly by the sensory register as images, almost like photographs. Auditory sensations are coded as sound patterns, similar to echoes. It may be that the other senses also have their own codes. Thus, for a second or so, a wealth of date from sensory experience remains intact. In these moments, we have a chance to select and organise information for further processing. Perception and attention are critical at this stage.

Attention

If every variation in colour, movement, sound, smell, temperature, and so on ended up in working memory, life would be impossible. By paying attention to selected stimuli and ignoring others, we limit the possibilities of processing. What we pay attention to is guided to a certain extent by what we already know and what we need to know. Thus, attention is involved in and influenced by all three memory process as shown in the earlier figure 5.1 (The information processing system). But attention takes effort and it is a limited resource. We can pay attention to only one cognitively demanding task at a time (Anderson *et al.*, 1985). But after years of practice, our attention and practice become automatic to perform multi-activities at one time i.e. driving car, listening to music, talking to friends, etc.

Attention plays an important role in teaching and learning process. The first step in learning is paying attention. Students cannot process information that they don't recognize or perceive. Many factors in the classroom influence student's attention. Eye catching or startling displays or actions can draw attention at the beginning of a lesson. Students have to maintain attention, stay focused on the important features of the learning situation.

Short Term Memory

Short term memory is memory that holds information received from the sensory register for up to about 30 seconds, although the length of the retention depends on a number of factors. It is a system for temporarily storing and managing information required to carry out complex cognitive tasks such as learning, reasoning and comprehension. Short term memory is involved in the selection, initiation and termination of information-processing functions such as encoding, storing and retrieving data.

One test of short term memory is memory span, the no. of items, usually words or numbers that a person can hold onto and recall. In a typical test of memory span, an examiner reads a list of random numbers aloud at about the rate of one number per second. At the end of a sequence, the person being tested is asked to recall the items in order. The average memory span for normal adults is 7 second. Short term memory is also termed recent or working memory. Baddeley (1986) stated that working memory is "the temporary storage of information that is being processed in any range of cognitive tasks".

Working memory is the "Workbench" of the memory system, the interface where new information is held temporarily and combined with knowledge from long-term memory. It "contains" what you are thinking about at the moment. For this reason, some psychologists consider the working memory to be synonymous with "consciousness" (Swaller *et al.*, 1998). The capacity of working memory is limited. It includes both temporary storage and active processing—the workbench of memory (Beddaley, 2001).

The sensory register holds sensory information for a few seconds, has a relatively large capacity, stores a copy of the sensory input, and loses information through a process involving the decay of the memory trace. Items in the sensory register that are attended to and recognised may be passed along to short-term memory. Short-term memory is different than working memory. It means first storage, the immediate memory for new information that can be held about 15 to 20 seconds (Baddaley, 2001). Early experiments suggested that the capacity of Short term memory was only about 5 to 9 separate new items at once (Miller, 1956). Later we will see that this limitation can be overcome by using strategies such as chunking or grouping, but 5 to 9 limit generally holds true in everyday life. It is quite common to remember a new phone number after looking it up, as you walk across the room to make the call. But two new phone numbers (14 digits) probably cannot be stored simultaneously. The type of information stored in short term memory consists of sounds, images, words, and information is lost from short term memory by being displaced by new inputs. Information in short term memory may be transferred to long term memory through either maintenance or elaborative rehearsal.

Long Term Memory

Long term memory contains words, sentences, ideas, concepts, and the life experiences we have had. The capacity of long term memory appears to be, for all practical purposes, unlimited. In addition, once information is securely stored in long term memory, it can remain there permanently. Our access to information in working memory is immediate because we are thinking about the information at that very moment. But access to information in long term memory requires time and effort. Recently, some psychologists have suggested that there are not two separate memory stores (working and long term). Rather working memory is the part of long term memory that works on (processes) currently activated information, so working memory is more about processing than storage (Wilson, 2001).

Clark and Palvio, (1991) suggested that information is stored in long term memory as either visual images or verbal units, or both. Psychologists, who agree with this point of view believe that information coded both visually and verbally is easiest to learn (Mayer and Sims, 1994). This may be one reason why explaining an idea with words and representing it visually in a figure, as we do in textbooks, has proved helpful to students (Mayer, 1999, 2001; Mantone and Mayer, 2001). But critics contend that the capacity of the brain is not large enough to store all the images we have seen or can imagine. They suggest that many images are actually stored as verbal codes and then translated into visual information when an image is needed (Schunk, 2000).

Another recent addition to the information processing model is the notion of long term working memory (Kintsch, 1998). Long term working memory holds the retrieval structures and strategies that pull from long-term memory the information needed at the moment. As we develop knowledge and expertise in an area, we create efficient long-term working memory structures for solving problems in that area.

(C) Intelligence

Psychology says no two individuals are alike. There exists individual differences and the major cause factor as studied by psychologists is "Intelligence". Stern (1914) defined intelligence as a general capacity of an individual to consciously adjust his thinking to new requirements. It is the general mental adaptability to new problems and conditions of life.

Thorndike (1914) stated that intelligence may be defined as the power of good responses from the point of view of truth or fact.

Wagnon (1937) viewed intelligence as the capacity to learn and adjust to relatively new and changing conditions.

Stoddard (1943) defined Intelligence as the ability to undertake activities that are difficult, complex and obstruct and which are adaptive to a goal and are done quickly and which have social value and which lead to the creation of something new and different.

Wechsler (1944) viewed that intelligence is the aggregate or global capacity of an individual to act purposefully, to think rationally and to deal effectively with his environment.

Woodworth and Marquis (1948) stated that intelligence means intellect put to use. It is the use of intellectual abilities for handling a situation or accomplishing any task.

Piaget (1952) viewed intelligence as the ability to adapt to one's surroundings.

Briggs (1962) Mitchell (1963), Keller (1964) found that intelligence was the major factor influencing academic achievement.

Freeman (1962) gave a comprehensive definition of intelligence:

- the adaptation or adjustment of individual to his environment
- the ability to learn
- the ability to carry out abstract thinking

Torrance (1965) concluded that more intelligent children with more capabilities are likely to accomplish more on academic tasks.

Sinha (1967) found that intelligence and academic achievement were significantly related beyond the 0.01 level of confidence.

Guilford (1967) gave a comprehensive model called the "Structure of Intellect", (SOI).

Lewis (1968) found intelligence and achievement to be highly correlated.

Berman (1970) found that exceptionally high achievement in final high school examination correlated significantly with high Intelligence Quotient.

Tyler (1974) pointed out that more intelligent children tend to get better grades in school, remain in school longer, and have more positive attitude towards school.

Srivastava (1974) found that intelligence is significantly correlated with academic achievement at 0.01 level of confidence.

Seetha (1975) reported that high achievers possessed superior intelligence when compared with low and non-achievers.

Contractor (1977) found that Intelligence Quotient was positively related with educational attainment.

Jarial (1981) reported that intelligence and academic achievements were positively and significantly related among the groups, males, females, arts and science and their intelligence and academic achievements were the functions of same mental operations, i.e. "convergent thinking".

Ameerjan (1981) in his model of determinants of academic achievement found that intelligence level is an important pupil variable for academic achievement.

Ingalls (1984) in a study observed that intelligence was a significant variable in achievement in mathematical concepts, reading and mathematical computation.

Sternberg (1985) stated that most of us have a pretty clear idea of what intelligence is. Intelligence, like love, is one of those concepts that are easier to recognise than to define. We often refer to other's intelligence describing people as bright, smart or quick on the one hand or as slow, dull or even stupid on the other. Most of us would agree that intelligence has something to do with the capacity to profit from experience and to adapt to relatively new situations. It is revealed that the person may be identified as intelligent, who

- reasons logically and well
- reads widely
- keeps an open mind
- is really smart
- is hard worker

Mohan and Bhatia (1985) revealed that superior psycho-motor performance was associated with higher intelligence.

Even after hundred years of research and theory on the nature of intelligence, there is still no clear definition of intelligence (Sternberg, 1988).

Neisser *et al.* (1996) viewed the term intelligence as an individual's abilities to understand complex ideas, to adapt effectively to the environment, to learn from experience, to engage in various forms of reasoning, to overcome obstacles by careful thought.

Jain (2003) viewed that intelligence is considered to be a set of abilities, the ability to learn quickly, the ability to solve difficult problems, the ability to perform tasks quickly and accurately, and so on. Ability allows a person to achieve a higher criterion of performance than someone else who lacks it.

Baron (2004) mentions that the ability that constitutes intelligence is generally useful in helping people achieve their goals, no matter what goals may be.

Influence of Environmental Factors on Intelligence

Genetic factors are definitely not the entire picture where human intelligence is concerned, however, other findings point to the conclusion that environmental variables, too, are important. One such finding is that performance on IQ tests has risen, substantially around the world at all age levels in recent decades. This phenomenon is known as the 'Flynn effects' after the name of a psychologist who first reported it (Flynn 1987, 1996). Such increases have averaged about 3IQ points per decade worldwide; but as shown in Figure 5.2 (below) in some countries, they have been even larger.

Additional evidence for the role of environmental factor in intelligence is provided by the findings of studies of environmental deprivation and environmental enrichment. With respect to deprivation, some findings suggest that intelligence can be reduced by the absence of key forms of environmental stimulation early in

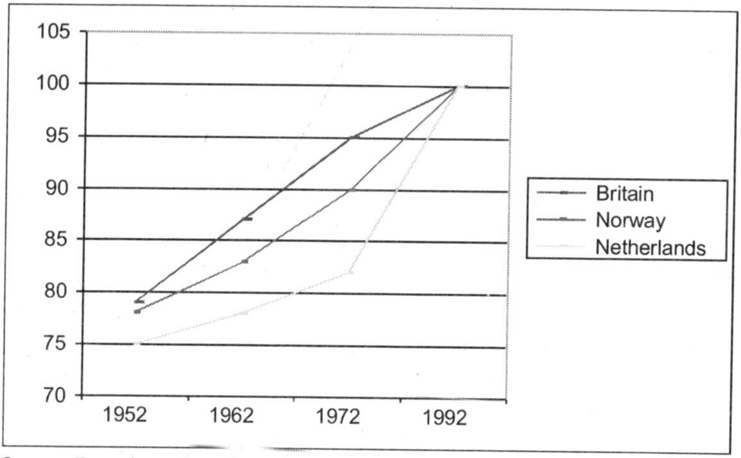

Source: Based on data from Flynn, 1999.

Fig 5.2: Influence of Environmental Factors on Intelligence

life (Gottfried, 1984). In terms of enrichment, removing children from sterile, restricted environments and placing them in more favourable settings seems to enhance their intellectual growth.

More carefully controlled efforts to increase intelligence through environmental interventions have produced beneficial results (Bryant and Maxwell, 1997); Gularnick, (1997). However Ramey and Ramey (1998) noted that such changes are most likely to occur when the following conditions are met, 1.) the interventions begin early and continue for a long time, 2.) the programmes are intense, involving home visits several times per week, 3.) the children receive new learning experiences delivered directly to them by experts rather than indirectly through their parents, 4.) the interventions are broad in scope, using many different procedures to enhance children development, 5.) the interventions are matched to the needs of individual children, and 6.) environmental supports (e.g. excellent schools) are put in place to support and maintain the positive attitudes of children towards learning. Needless to say, programmes that meet these criteria tend to be expensive. But they can also yield important financial benefits; for instance, one study cited by Ramey and Ramey (1998) suggests that appropriate early intervention programmes might have prevented more than 300,000 children in the United States alone from developing IQs that placed them in the 'mentally retarded' category (i.e., IQs below 70). Given that such children often require extensive corrective assistance and training, the potential savings to be realised through early enrichment might well be substantial. So there are strong economic arguments, as well as social and humanitarian ones for intervention programmes a given society can afford.

Additional support for the role of environmental factors in intelligence is provided by the finding that many biological factors that children encounter while growing up can affect their intelligence. Prolonged malnutrition can adversely affect IQ (Sigman, 1995), and use of alcohol and drugs too may affect the health of developing foetuses by affecting their intelligence adversely (Neisser *et al.*, 1996).

There is a considerable evidence that both environmental and genetic factors play a role in intelligence. Different studies (Plomin, 1997; Neisser *et al.*, 1996) seem to favour the view that genetic factors may account for more of the variance in IQ scores within a given population than environmental factors. But many people and psychologists have been made somewhat uneasy by this conclusion in the past because they assumed that heritable characteristics that are strongly influenced by genetic factors cannot be readily changed. It's important to recognise that this assumption is false. For instance, height is a characteristic which is highly heritable, influenced by genetic factors to a greater extent than by intelligence. Yet despite this fact, average heights have increased in many countries as nutrition has improved. The fact that a trait is strongly influenced by genetic factors does not imply that it cannot be affected by environmental factors as well (Baron, 2004).

Singh *et al.* (2012) reported that one month practice of meditation reduced psychological stress responses and improved cognitive functions, and the effects were pronounced with practice of meditation for a longer duration. Naik *et al.* (2016) found that there is a positive effect of *Rajyoga* Meditation on Intelligence Quotient of Attention Deficit Hyperactivity Disorder.

6

Yoga: A Way to Holistic Education

Research Module, Results and Educational Implications

As mentioned earlier about the research study done by the author, various private schools of Jalandhar city and the cantonement area affiliated to CBSE, having more or less same infrastructure, student strength and human resources, were identified. After scrutinizing these schools, the investigator interacted with the Principals of these schools to get their permission to conduct the experiment in their schools for research purpose. After consistent efforts, the investigator got acceptance from eight public schools. From each school, students of IX class were selected for the present investigation. Initially available sections from the schools were taken. The investigator started her experiment with 800 students from eight public schools of Jalandhar.

Tools

The following standardised and self-developed tools were administered to collect data:

1. A Value Orientation Programme and Yoga Module (developed by the Investigator)
2. Bisht Battery of Stress Scales (BBSS) (Bisht, 1987)
3. PGI Memory Scale for Concentration (Pershad and Wig, 1994)
4. Short Term Memory Test (APRC, 1978)
5. Raven's Progressive Matrices and Vocabulary Scales (Raven *et al.*, 1983)

6. Academic Achievement Tests (developed by the Investigator)

Procedure

Bisht Battery of Stress Scales was administered to the students of selected schools to classify them into high and low stress by considering their academic and achievement stress. On the basis of the stress scores, 30 per cent students with high stress and 30 per cent students with low stress were identified and selected for further study.

High stress students were divided into two groups i.e. 50 per cent students were allotted to experimental group and another 50 per cent students were allotted to control group. The same procedure was followed for the low stress students.

After the allotment of the students in experimental group and control group, concentration test, intelligence test, memory test and academic performance tests were administered to the students of experimental group as well as control group prior to the start of the experiment. Value orientation programme alongwith yoga module was executed in the experimental group, whereas the students in the control group did not get the yoga treatment. After seven weeks of yoga intervention, same set of the tests were again administered to the students of experimental as well as control group. After scoring, the statistical treatment was given.

Design of the Study

The design of the study was envisaged in five parts:

(i) 2 × 2 factorial design was employed on the adjusted gain scores of concentration, memory, intelligence and academic performance. In the present study, adjusted gain scores have been preferred over simple gain scores, because many a times, simple gain scores are misleading. A student who achieves 30 marks in pre-test and attains 60 marks in post- test, yields gain scores of 30 marks. Whereas another student who scores 80 marks in pre-test and attains 95 marks in post-test, yields gain scores of 15 marks. In this situation, it seems as if the strength of experiment in the first situation was higher than in the second situation, which is misleading because amount of effort one requires to move from

30 marks to 60 marks would be definitely less than the amount of effort one requires to move from 80 marks to 95 marks. As we move higher, increase of every single mark requires more and more effort. Therefore, to minimize this error due to absolute marks difference, the investigator preferred the use of adjusted gain scores over simple gain scores.

In this research design, concentration was studied as a dependent variable, whereas stress was studied as an independent variable and was used for the purpose of classification: High Stress and Low Stress. On the other hand, Yoga treatment was studied as independent variable and was manipulated to experimental group. Control group was not given any treatment.

The schematic layout of the design on the adjusted gain scores of concentration is presented below in the Fig.6.1:

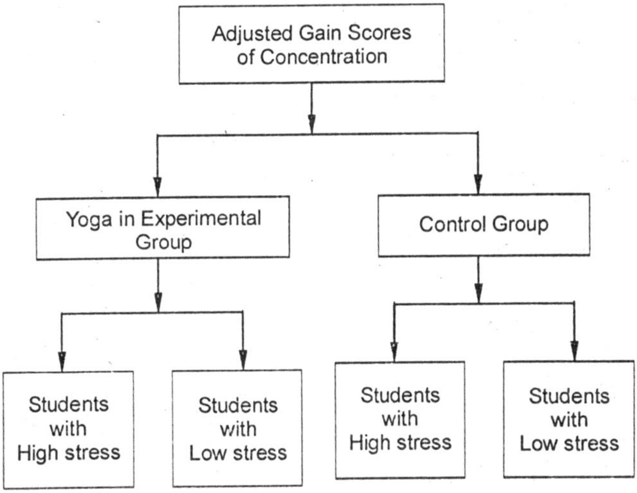

Fig. 6.1: The Schematic Representation of the 2×2 Factorial Design on the Adjusted Gain Scores of Concentration

(i) Same design was replicated on the adjusted gain scores of Memory, Intelligence and Academic Performance.

(ii) Similar design was replicated on the adjusted gain scores of different antecedents of academic performance, i.e. Social Science, Mathematics and Science.

Qualitative analysis was also carried out to study the variations regarding the effect of yoga on academic performance in Social Studies, Mathematics and Science.

The collected data was grouped taking percentage of marks as class intervals and number of students falling in those class intervals as frequencies. Cumulative frequencies and thereafter the cumulative frequency percentages were computed for each class interval for the purpose of drawing More than Ogive. This procedure was followed for pre-tests and post-tests of experimental as well as control groups for high stress and low stress groups. Difference in cumulative frequency percentages of pre-tests and post-tests of experimental and control group was also computed for comparison purposes.

Preparation of a Value Orientation Programme and a Yoga Module

Following domains of human personality were considered for planning of a yoga module:

1. Physical Health
2. Mental Well being
3. Intellectual Development
4. Social Adjustability
5. Emotional Maturity
6. Moral Upliftment
7. Spiritual Growth

These domains are interrelated, interdependent and jointly enrich human personality. Discussions were done with yoga experts and their valuable suggestions were given a practical shape. Seven themes (week wise) were prepared in accordance with seven domains.

The themes are as follows:

(i) Mind Body Relationship
(ii) Self-Discipline
(iii) Social Responsibility
(iv) Positive Values
(v) Moral Upliftment
(vi) Social and Moral Values
(vii) Personality Development (Body, Mind and Soul)

Table 6.1: Day Wise Objectives Corresponding to Themes

WEEK 1	THEME: MIND BODY RELATIONSHIP
Day 1	To develop habit of early rising.
Day 2	To develop awareness about personal hygiene and physical fitness.
Day 3	To motivate students for daily prayer.
Day 4	To create awareness about right posture.
Day 5	To inculcate respect towards elders.
Day 6	To develop appreciation about time management.
WEEK 2	**THEME: SELF DISCIPLINE**
Day 1	To create consciousness towards their duty.
Day 2	To develop democratic and scientific attitude.
Day 3	To inculcate habit of cleanliness.
Day 4	To develop good study habits.
Day 5	To inculcate habit of respecting teachers.
Day 6	To make them aware of right eating habits.
WEEK 3	**THEME: SOCIAL RESPONSIBILITY**
Day 1	To develop the feeling of true patriotism.
Day 2	To make them conscious about their social duties.
Day 3	To make them realize about the relevance of society.
Day 4	To make them innovative for social progress.
Day 5	To develop the art of appreciation towards Indian culture.
Day 6	To develop 'we feeling' among the students.
WEEK 4	**THEME: POSITIVE VALUES**
Day 1	To encourage them for truthful living.
Day 2	To develop right and positive attitude.
Day 3	To motivate them for self-control.
Day 4	To develop a sense of dignity of labour.
Day 5	To create an interest in selfless activities.
WEEK 5	**THEME: MORAL UPLIFTMENT**
Day 1	To encourage the students to become judicious minded.
Day 2	To develop optimism among them.
Day 3	To develop their will power.
Day 4	To make them realize the significance of self-confidence.
Day 5	To develop a sense of togetherness.
Day 6	To realize oneness with Almighty.
WEEK 6	**THEME: SOCIAL AND MORAL VALUES**
Day 1	To make them believe in themselves.
Day 2	To develop a feeling of secularism.
Day 3	To inculcate faith in future.
Day 4	To inspire them to become effective citizens.
Day 5	To help them to make proper use of their leisure time.
Day 6	To develop appreciation towards flora and fauna
WEEK: 7	**THEME: PERSONALITY DEVELOPMENT (BODY + MIND + SOUL)**
Day 1	To encourage them for hard work.
Day 2	To help them to realize the presence of infinite energy.
Day 3	To develop positive attitude.
Day 4	To create an awareness about all round development of personality.
Day 5	To inculcate the habit of self-learning.
Day 6	To make them realize the power of determination.

Table 6.2: Final Draft of Weekly Chart of a Value Orientation Programme and Yoga Module

Week-1: Theme—Mind-Body Relationship

Day→	*1*	*2*	*3*	*4*	*5*	*6*
Objectives	To understand Body, Mind and Soul	To develop the relationship between mental state and body actions	To study effect of mental state on body actions	To understand effect of body actions on the mental state	To understand the effect of Body-Mind coordination on the performance (Decision making)	To understand the effect of Body Mind coordination on performance (Memory, Achievement)
Daily orientation talk	The investigator mentions daily about the mind-body relationship with the help of different examples and situations. She further elaborates about the significance of Body-Mind coordination. She daily concludes her programme by again focusing on the theme, i.e. Mind-Body Relationship and urges the subjects to practically experience it.					
Yoga intervention programme	Yoga Asanas = 35 m Sukshm Vyaam = 20 m. Padmasana = 1 m. Deep Breathing = 5 m 'Om Dhvani = 1 m (3 times) Gaytri Mantra = 1 m. Trikonasana = 2 m. Tadasana = 3 m. Shavasana = 2 m Pranayama = 10 m. Deep Breathing = 2 m. Anulom Vilom = 4 m. Bhaamari = 4m. Meditation = 5 m Dhyana on 'OM' = 4 m. Prayer = 1 m.	SV = 20 m Padmasana = 1 m. Deep Breathing = 5 m 'Om' = 1 m Gaytri Mantra = 1 m Trikonasana = 2 m Tadasana = 2 m. Shavasana = 3 m Pranayama = 10 m Meditation = 5 m (Dhayana)	SV = 18 m Padmasana = 1 m Deep Breathing = 4 m 'Om' = 1 m Gaytri Mantra = 1 m Trikonasana = 2 m Tadasana = 2 m Vajrasana = 2 m Shavasana = 4 m Pranayam = 10 m Meditation = 5 m	SV = 15 m Padmasana = 1 m Deep Breathing = 4 m 'Om' = 1 m Gaytri Mantra = 1 m Trikonasana = 2 m Tadasana = 2 m Vajrasana = 2 m Makrasana = 3 m Shavasana = 4 m Pranayama = 10 m Meditation = 5m	SV = 12 m Padmasana = 1 m Deep Breathing = 4 m 'Om' = 1 m Gaytri Mantra = 1 m Suryanamaskar = 6 m Shavasana = 2 m Tadasana = 2 m Vajrasana = 1 m Makrasana = 2 m Shavasana = 3 m Pranayama = 10 m Meditation = 5 m	Same as on Friday and Suryanamaskar is learnt.

	On the first day students are oriented for the basic asanas, pranayama and meditation. The investigator demonstrates each and every asana to the students. They are simultaneously explained the benefits of each asana. Every asana is monitored and an effort is made to do the asanas correctly. This process continues and a new asana is added after 2 days when the students' body gets adapted to the earlier ones and their body becomes flexible. Duration of asanas is also adjusted as the days proceed. Demonstrations are given daily with the help of a yoga instructor as well as investigator herself. When the students perform, the investigator always tries to correlate the asana, pranayama and dhyana with the objective of the day while focussing on the theme of the week in general. On the first day, the investigator correlates the asanas with the body's well-being, Pranayama for stability of mind and Dhyana for peace of soul. Sukhsma Vyaam, Trikonasana, Tadasana are done to keep the body healthy and strong. Deep Breathing, 'Om' dhvani, Shavasana are done for mental calmness. Dhyana, prayers and Gayatri mantras are done to connect with the inner self. On the second day, the investigator trains and also ascertains that students feel the change and relaxation in their mental and physical setup, while performings Shavasana, deep breathing and dhyana. On the third day, the investigator selects a few students, who have mastered the asanas. Having learnt the art of various yogasanas, the selected students realize its benefits and also feel the oneness of mind and body. Since their mind is one with their body, they can perform better. Those students who take the asanas lightly and whose body and mind are not well coordinated, cannot perform in the correct posture. Time and again, the investigator continues to motivate and encourage them to excel in their asanas by working at the level of their thought processes. The same approach is adopted for the next three days. Gradually, the students lagging behind in their performance also pick up and start performing well; their mind and body coordination improves which helps them in taking right decisions. This is also correlated with the objective of Suryanamaskar performed on the fifth day. This comprises 12 asanas which the students learn through demonstration. It also highlights the objective of the sixth day.					
Value Orientation programme (10 minutes daily)	Lecture based on situational references for Body, Mind and Soul	Story of Shaheed Bhagat Singh, Nadirshah and Saint talk	Story of martyrdom of 5th Sikh Guru Shri Arjun Dev ji, Life History of Mother Teresa	Story of king Ashokas Kalinga war and few examples.	Story of Dr Shareen Irani-life achievement, and example of Napolean.	Story of Swami Vivekananda showing his reading and memory abilities.

Weak-2: Theme—Self Discipline

Day →	*1*	*2*	*3*	*4*	*5*	*6*
Objectives	To make them aware of personal hygiene and physical fitness	To guide them about self-control	To promote vegetarianism	To develop sound study habits.	To make them aware of Time Management	To inculcate habit of respecting their teachers

Daily orientation talk	The investigator daily flows the idea that healthy mind and body setup can attain self-discipline, provided above mentioned objectives are achieved. For this purpose, daily orientation talk includes stress on their living, diet, time planning, control over senses, sound study habits etc. An effort is made to bring positive behavioural change in the personality of the students.					
Yoga Intervention Programme	S.V.—10 m Padmasana—1m Deep Breathing—3 m 'Om'—1m G.M.—1m Trikonasana—2m Suryanamasker—5m Shavasana—2m Tadasana—2m Vajrasana—1m Bhujangasana—2m Shallabhasana—2m Shavasana—3m Pranayama—10m Meditation—5m	S.V.—10 m Padmasana—1m Deep Breathing—2 m 'Om'—1m G.M.—1m Suryanamasker—5m Shavasana—2m Tadasana—2m Vajrasana—1m Bhujangasana—2m Shallabhasana—2m Makrasana—2m Shavasana—4m Pranayama—10m Meditation—5m	S.V.—8m Padmasana—1m Deep Breathing—2 m 'Om'—1m G.M.—1m Suryanamasker—5m Shavasana—2m Tadasana—1½ m Vajrasana—1m Ushtrasana—1½ m Bhujangasana—2m Shallabhasana—2m Pawanmukta-asana—1½ m Makrasana—1½ m Shavasana—4m Pranayama—10m Meditation—5m	S.V.—8m Padmasana—1m Deep Breathing—2 m 'Om'—1m G.M.—1m Suryanamasker—5m Shavasana—2m Tadasana—1½ m Vajrasana—1m Ushtrasana—1½ m Shashankasana-1½m Bhujangasana—1½ m Shallabhasana—1½ m Pawanmukta-asana-1½ m Makrasana—1½ m Shavasana—3 ½ m Pranayama—10m Meditation—5m	S.V.—8m Padmasana—1m Deep Breathing—2 m 'Om'—1m G.M.—1m Suryanamasker—5m Shavasana—2m Tadasana—1½ m Vajrasana—1m Ushtrasana—1½ m Shashankasana-1½m Bhujangasana—1½ m Shallabhasana—1½ m Pawanmukta-asana-1½ m Makrasana—1½ m Shavasana—3 ½ m Pranayama—10m Meditation—5m	S.V.—8m Padmasana—1m Deep Breathing—2 m 'Om'—1m G.M.—1m Suryanamasker—5m Shavasana—2m Tadasana—1½ m Vajrasana—1m Ushtrasana—1½ m Shashankasana-1½m Bhujangasana—1½ m Shallabhasana—1½ m Pawanmukta-asana-1½ m Makrasana—1½ m Shavasana—3 ½ m Pranayama—10m Meditation—5m
	New asanas are added in the 2nd week. Investigator demonstrates every asana and simultaneously students too perform it. Regular monitoring is done side by side. Explanation is delivered while the students perform asanas, pranayama and dhyana. A continuous effort is made to maintain the connectivity of students with their inner being. Throughout the yoga session, it is repeatedly instructed to keep eyes closed in order to stop the wastage of their energy through sense of seeing. On the first day, focus is on their personal hygiene and physical fitness. While performing asanas, it is explained by the investigator about the significance of physical cleanliness, nail cutting, proper food intake at proper time. Investigator also asks the students about their favourite food items. Most of them express their liking for 'fast food and cold drinks'. The investigator cautions them about the ill effects of fast food and cold drinks. The benefit of each asanas is explained. When vajrasana is performed, the students are informed about its benefit, which is quick digestion.					

	On the second day, the objective of self-control is targeted by educating and training the students while performing tadasana, bhujangasana, deepbreathing, etc. The students are explained how during pranayama and shavasana, they should focus their attention on their breath. While chanting gayatri mantra and 'Om' dhvani, they are taught to concentrate continuously on the words spoken by them. This whole process enables them to learn about self-control and helps their body and mind to get trained for it. This idea is strengthened further by value orientation programmes. On the third day, students are told to observe their breathing speed. This varies from student to student. They report it as 'very fast', 'somewhat fast' and 'not very smooth'. They are also informed about the benefits of vegetarian diet while doing gayatri mantra, om dhvani and prayer. The investigator also focuses on the omnipresence of the Almighty, as the controller of every force. It is explained to the students that eating has direct link with the mental framework: "When we are angry, full of jealousy or in a hurry, our breath moves fast and it is not good for our health." The investigator also explains about the benefits of deep breathing and the actual breathing pattern of a common person. Rishi Patanjali prescribed vegetarian diet for better results of yoga. The fourth day lays emphasis on sound study habits, which can be attained through yogasanas. Bhujangasana improves concentration and memory and so do deep breathing, shavasana, pranayama and dhyan. Sound sleep refreshes the body cells and improves the whole system. Pure oxygen intake during pranayama improves blood circulation and throws out toxins of the body. Asanas increase flexibility of the back bone, helping the blood to flow frequently and smoothly towards the brain improving memory of the practitioner. It also helps in maintaining a right posture. The concept of Time Management is included in yogic practice. The entire programme is planned for an hour on daily basis: yoga asanas—35 minutes, pranayama—10 minutes, dhyan—5 minutes, lecture—10 minutes. Besides, the students are also taught to respect their elders and teachers. Change in behaviour is a gradual process, which comes after a long term practice.					
Value Orientation programme	Story from Swami Vivekananda's life, harmful effects of junk food	Situational references from their day-to-day living.	Lecture on difference between animal and human physiology, story quoted from Sadhu Vaswani's book.	Life history of scientist Praful Chander Roy.	Story of a boy going with a diamond to a Jeweller.	Eklavya's story showing an unconditional surrender and dedication towards his Guru.

WEEK-3: Theme—Social Responsibility

Day→	1	2	3	4	5	6
Objectives	To realize them about the relevance of social environment	To inculcate the spirit of universal brotherhood	To develop a feeling of compassion among the students	To create appreciation towards Indian culture	To inculcate respect for social and cultural heritage	To provide respect for great nationalists
Daily orientation talk	The investigator explains the students about the significance of healthy social environment, since man is a social animal. Certain values are elaborately discussed to motivate them to contribute productively to the society, which helps them in becoming effective social beings. They are also apprised of their cultural moorings. Thanksgiving prayer is recited daily to get the students connected with the Ultimate.					

Yoga intervention programme	Suksham Vyaam = 5 m. Padmasana = 1 m. Deep Breathing = 2 m 'Om' Dhwani = 1 m Gaytri Mantra = 1 m Suryanamaskar = 5m Shavasana = 2m. Tadasana = 1 ½ m. Navasana = 3 m Konasana = 2 m Vajrasana = 1m Bhujangasana = 1 ½ m Shallabhasana = 1 ½ m Padotanasana = 1 ½ m Pawanmuktasana = 2m Shavasana = 4m Pranayama = 10m Meditation = 5 m	Suksham Vyaam = 5 m. Padmasana = 1 m. Deep Breathing = 2 m 'Om' Dhvani = 1 m Gaytri Mantra = 1 m Suryanamaskar = 5m Shavasana = 2m. Tadasana = 1 ½ m. Navasana = 3 m Konasana = 2 m Vajrasana = 1m Bhujangasana = 1 ½ m Shallabhasana = 1 ½ m Padotanasana = 1 ½ m Pawanmuktasana = 2m Shavasana = 4m Pranayama = 10m Meditation = 5 m	Suksham Vyaam = 5 m. Padmasana = 1 m. Deep Breathing = 2 m 'Om' Dhvani = 1 m Gaytri Mantra = 1 m Suryanamaskar = 5m Shavasana = 2m. Tadasana = 1 ½ m. Navasana = 3 m Konasana = 2 m Vajrasana = 1m Bhujangasana = 1 ½ m Shallabhasana = 1 ½ m Padctanasana = 1 ½ m Pawanmuktasana = 2m Shavasana = 4m Pranayama = 10m Meditation = 5 m	Suksham Vyaam = 4 m. Padmasana = 1 m. Deep Breathing = 2 m 'Om' Dhvani = 1 m Gaytri Mantra = 1 m Suryanamaskar = 5m Shavasana = 2m. Tadasana = 1 m. Navasana = 2 m Konasana = 1 ½ m Vajrasana = 1m Bhujangasana = 1 ½ m Shallabhasana = 1 ½ m Makrasana = 1 ½ m Chakraasana = 3m Hastpadotanasana = 2m Shavasana = 4m Pranayama = 10m Meditation = 5 m	Suksham Vyaam = 4 m. Padmasana = 1 m. Deep Breathing = 2 m 'Om' Dhvani = 1 m Gaytri Mantra = 1 m Suryanamaskar = 5m Shavasana = 2m. Tadasana = 1 m. Navasana = 2 m Konasana = 1 ½ m Vajrasana = 1m Bhujangasana = 1 ½ m Shallabhasana = 1 ½ m Makrasana = 1 ½ m Chakraasana = 3m Hastpadotanasana = 2m Shavasana = 4m Pranayama = 10m Meditation = 5 m	Suksham Vyaam = 4 m. Padmasana = 1 m. Deep Breathing = 2 m 'Om' Dhvani = 1 m Gaytri Mantra = 1 m Suryanamaskar = 5m Shavasana = 2m. Tadasana = 1 m. Navasana = 2 m Konasana = 1 ½ m Vajrasana = 1m Bhujangasana = 1 ½ m Shallabhasana = 1 ½ m Makrasana = 1 ½ m Chakraasana = 3m Hastpadotanasana = 2m Shavasana = 4m Pranayama = 10m Meditation = 5 m
	As any classroom is a miniature form of society, the investigator trains the students for yoga package in a social environment, including students from different sections of the society. When the students chant 'Om' dhvani, the collective sound of a group or a class makes the environment pure and peaceful. Positive energy travels in the environment, which is beneficial for each participant. The trainer correlates it with a similie by explaining that if the social environment is healthy and peaceful, each individual will grow in a positive manner. New and difficult asanas are added gradually, as the flexibility in the bodies of participants increase day by day. Students perform asanas collectively and get motivated by their peer group, which inculcates and develops social values in them. Same asanas are repeated for another two days. Each asana carries numerous benefits. It help the students to be tolerant. As the breathing pattern improves gradually, the adamant attitude decreases. The feeling of compassion is inculcated, when anger is reduced with the help of yogasana, pranayama and meditation. Daily prayer inculcates a feeling of gratitude and surrender among the students. They get inspired to become better social beings. For the next three days, new asanas are added. A sequence is followed from simple to difficult. The complete yoga programme comes from our rich cultural heritage, from Rishi Patanjali and other great ancient saints. The students are told to feel honoured and be proud of being Indian. The technique of asanas, pranayama and meditation are totally scientific, which is transferred to the learners by correlating the relevance of yoga to the modern scientific period.					

Day→	1	2	3	4	5	6
Value Orientation programme	Story of two parrots and news of a child growing with a fox in Lucknow.	Story of Swami Vivekananda and his Muslim fellow	Contribution of Bhagat Puran Singh and story of Japanese soldiers	Story of Pakistani Brigadier	Lecture on the general examples about richness of culture like Yoga, Vastu, Ayurveda, etc.	Story of Keshavra v Baliram Hedgevar

WEEK-4: Theme—Positive Values

Contd...

Day→	1	2	3	4	5	6
Objectives	To motivate them to adopt the idea of Non-violence	To encourage the students to become fearless and truthful	To understand and appreciate the relevance of peace in society	To inculcate a sense of dignity of labour	To encourage the students for Honest living	To motivate the students to participate in selfiess service
Daily orientation talk	Inculcation of positive values go a long way in building a good character of an individual. The investigator imparts healthy values among the students on regular basis through general talk, yoga session and value orientation programmes. Skill of stimulus-variation and question-answer technique are followed to make an impact.					
Yoga intervention programme	Suksham Vyaam = 3 m. Padmasana = 1 m Deep Breathing = 2 m 'Om' Dhvani = 1 m Gaytri Mantra = 1 m Suryanamaskar = 5m Shavasana = 2m Navasana = 2 m Janushirasana = 3m Konasana = 1 ½ m Vajrasana = 1m Bhujangasana = 1 ½ m Chakrasana 2 ½ m Hastpadotasna = 1 ½ m Halasana = 2 m Matsyanasana = 2 m Shavasana = 3m	Suksham Vyaam = 3 m. Padmasana = 1 m Deep Breathing = 2 m 'Om' Dhvani = 1 m Gaytri Mantra = 1 m Suryanamaskar = 5m Shavasana = 2m Navasana = 2 m Janushirasana = 3m Konasana = 1 ½ m Vajrasana = 1m Bhujangasana = 1 ½ m Chakrasana 2 ½ m Hastpadotasna = 1 ½ m Halasana = 2 m Matsyanasana = 2 m Shavasana = 4m	Suksham Vyaam = 3 m. Padmasana = 1 m Deep Breathing = 2 m 'Om' Dhvani = 1 m Gaytri Mantra = 1 m Suryanamaskar = 5m Shavasana = 2m Navasana = 2 m Janushirasana = 3m Konasana = 1 ½ m Vajrasana = 1m Bhujangasana = 1 ½ m Chakrasana 2 ½ m Hastpadotasna = 1 ½ m Halasana = 2 m Matsyanasana = 2 m Shavasana = 4m	Suksham Vyaam = 2m. Padmasana = 1 m Deep Breathing = 2 m 'Om' Dhvani = 1 m Gaytri Mantra = 1 m Suryanamaskar = 5m Shavasana = 2m Navasana = 2 m Paschmotasana = 3m Konasana = 2 m Vajrasana = 1m Bhujangasana = 2 m Chakrasana = 2 m Hastpadotanasana = 1½m Halasana = 2m Matsyanasana = 2m Shavasana = 3 ½ m	Suksham Vyaam = 2m. Padmasana = 1 m Deep Breathing = 2 m 'Om' Dhvani = 1 m Gaytri Mantra = 1 m Suryanamaskar = 5m Shavasana = 2m Navasana = 2 m Paschmotasana = 3m Konasana = 2 m Vajrasana = 1m Bhujangasana = 2 m Chakrasana = 2 m Hastpadotanasana = 1½m Halasana = 2m Matsyanasana = 2m	Suksham Vyaam = 2m. Padmasana = 1 m Deep Breathing = 2 m 'Om' Dhvani = 1 m Gaytri Mantra = 1 m Suryanamaskar = 5m Shavasana = 2m Navasana = 2 m Paschmotasana = 3m Konasana = 2 m Vajrasana = 1m Bhujangasana = 2 m Chakrasana = 2 m Hastpadotanasana = 1½m Halasana = 2m Matsyasana = 2m Shavasana = 3 ½ m

	Pranayama = 10m Meditation = 5 m	Pranayama = 10m Meditation = 5 m	Pranayama = 10m Meditation = 5 m	Pranayama = 10m Meditation = 5 m	Shavasana = 3 ½ m Pranayama = 10m Meditation = 5 m	Pranayama = 10m Meditation = 5 m
	The students start practicing difficult asanas from the fourth week. As the days advance, the ability or capacity of the students to perform the different asanas, including breathing exercise and dhyana gets better. Simultaneously, positive values are also absorbed and accepted by them easily and naturally. Since yoga package carries numerous advantages, the investigator focuses on the various aspects of excellent performance of the asanas, pranayama and dhyana techniques. For the first three days, same set of asanas are performed. The schedule of yogasana is the same every day. Pranayama and dhyana are performed daily. The concept of non-violence is explained on regular basis by the investigator. The students are also informed about the type of diet they should have in order to experience the good effect of the yogasanas. While performing shavasana, the investigator talks about the energy that can be tapped from the Cosmos and the Ultimate force. The yogic practice leads the practitioner to the world of peace, where no fear and violence exist. They become calm and peaceful internally. The students share their personal experiences of yogic asanas with the investigator at the end of the session daily. They also report about their parents' observations regarding the behavioural changes in them due to the practice of yoga. During the last three days of yogic exercises, one more asana is added which helps in making the body and internal organs of the students healthy and strong. Overall yoga motivates the learner to live a contented and honest life, and also develops in them the faith in selfless service. Deep breathing makes the mind stable and facilitates positive thought process. Meditation connects a person to nothinglessness or 'Shunya' and consequently helps him/her in shedding ego.					
Day→	**1**	**2**	**3**	**4**	**5**	**6**
Value Orientation programme	Story of a Dacoit Anguleemal	Story of George Washington and Alexander	Story of India—Pakistan war, A story of Alfred Nobel.	Story of Dr. A.P.J. Abdul Kalam's childhood, A story of three persons hitting a stone	News item of abduction of Hoshiarpur (Punjab, India) boy Abhi Verma	Story of Ishwar Chander Vidyasagar

WEEK-5: Theme—Moral Upliftment

Day→	**1**	**2**	**3**	**4**	**5**	**6**
Objectives	To enlighten them about the significance of truthful living	To make them aware of negative impact of jealousy	To encourage them to become judicious minded	To develop an attitude of helping others	To help the students to make their will power strong	To promote an idea of selfless service
Daily orientation talk	Regular efforts are made to inculcate good values to uplift the students morally. A strong message is conveyed to them that unless they follow right values, they cannot be considered real human beings. It is through different orientation programmes that valuable attributes are taught to the learners.					

Yoga intervention programme	Suksha m Vyaa m = 2 m. Pad masana = 1 m Deep Breathing = 2 m 'O m' Dhvani = 1 m Gaytri Mantra = 1 m Suryana maskar = 5 m Shavasana = 2 m Navasana = 2 m Paschmotanasana = 3 m Konasana = 2 m Vajrasana = 1 m Bhujangasana = 2 m Chakrasana 2 m Sarvangasana = 3 m Matsyanasana = 2 m Shavasana = 4 m Pranaya ma = 10 m Meditation = 5 m	Suksha m Vyaa m = 2 m. Pad masana = 1 m Deep Breathing = 2 m 'O m' Dhvani = 1 m Gaytri Mantra = 1 m Suryana maskar = 5 m Shavasana = 2 m Navasana = 2 m Pasch motanasana = 3 m Konasana = 2 m Vajrasana = 1 m Bhujangasana = 2 m Chakrasana = 2 m Sarvangasana = 3 m Matsyanasana = 2 m Shavasana = 4 m Pranaya ma = 10 m Meditation = 5 m	Suksha m Vyaa m = 2 m. Pad masana = 1 m Deep Breathing = 2 m 'O m' Dhvani = 1 m Gaytri Mantra = 1 m Suryana maskar = 5 m Shavasana = 2 m Navasana = 2 m Pasch motanasana = 3 m Konasana = 2 m Vajrasana = 1 m Bhujangasana = 2 m Chakrasana 2 m Sarvangasana = 3 m Matsyanasana = 2 m Shavasana = 4 m Pranaya ma = 10 m Meditation = 5 m	Suksha m Vyaa m = 2 m. Pad masana = 1 m Deep Breathing = 2 m 'O m' Dhvani = 1 m Gaytri Mantra = 1 m Suryana maskar = 5 m Shavasana = 2 m Navasana = 2 m Pasch motanasana = 3 m Konasana = 2 m Vajrasana = 1 m Bhujangasana = 2 m Chakrasana 2 m Sarvangasana = 3 m Matsyanasana = 2 m Shavasana = 4 m Pranaya ma = 10 m Meditation = 5 m	Suksha m Vyaa m = 2 m. Pad masana = 1 m Deep Breathing = 2 m O m' Dhvani = 1 m Gaytri Mantra = 1 m Suryana maskar = 5 m Shavasana = 2 m Navasana = 2 m Pasch motanasana = 3 m Konasana = 2 m Vajrasana = 1 m Bhujangasana = 2 m Chakrasana 2 m Sarvangasana = 3 m Matsyanasana = 2 m Shavasana = 4 m Pranaya ma = 10 m Meditation = 5 m	Suksha m Vyaa m = 2 m. Pad masana = 1 m O m Dhvani = 2 m 'O m' Dhva m = 1 m Gaytri Mantra = 1 m Suryana maskar = 5 m Shavasana = 2 m Navasana = 2 m Paschmotanasana = 3 m Konasana = 2 m Vajrasana = 1 m Bhujangasana = 2 m Chakrasana = 2 m Sarvangasana = 3 m Matsyanasana = 2 m Shavasana = 4 m Pranaya ma = 10 m Meditation = 5 m
	As discussed earlier in detail about advantages of yoga programme, investigator prepares a set pattern of whole yoga package which is to be followed as such for the rest of the period, i.e. 5th, 6th and the 7th week. Attention of the students is focused on the inculcation of above said values through yoga package. Objectives are repeated in order to fix the idea in their mind and also to make them realize about the relevance of these values for their moral development. All ideas are endorsed with the help of a value orientation programme.					
Day→	**1**	**2**	**3**	**4**	**5**	**6**
Value Orientation programme	Story of Socrates	Story of Dr. Rajendra Prasad, story of Shivaji	Story of Vinoba Bhave, story of Justice Raman	Story of Mahatma Gandhi, story of Sh. Lal Bahadur Shastri	Stories of Mihir Sen, Thomas Edison	Story of Sh. Lal Bahadur Shastri

WEEK-6: Theme—Social and Moral Values

Day→	1	2	3	4	5	6
Objectives	To make them realize about the relevance of 'Self Determination' for achieving aim.	To develop the feeling of gratitude towards Almighty	To realize the significance of Honesty	To motivate students to utilize their energy purposefully	To make the students aware of Indian culture	To enable the students to perform their duty sincerely and judiciously
Daily orientation talk	Daily Thanksgiving prayer is recited by the investigator along with the students. Daily chanting of Gaytri Mantra with its meaning is done in the class, which makes them mentally and spiritually strong. It prepares a solid foundation of a value culture in the personality of the students.					
Yoga intervention programme	**SAME SET OF YOGA INTERVENTION PROGRAMME OF WEEK 5 IS BEING FOLLOWED**					
	The investigator makes all efforts to strengthen each and every aspect of the learners through yoga. As a result, they develop good mental and physical strength to perform asanas, pranayama and dhyana. They daily report about the changes taking place in their physical, mental and spiritual levels. Few of them also report about their reduced anger and restlessness. Some students also share about improvement in their appetite and sleep. It is observed that their memory and concentration also improve. Some of them had started performing 'Om' dhvani and bhramari pranayama before doing their homework in the evening. The also become more conscious of Indian culture and tradition. The following value orientation programme facilitate the investigator in imparting social and moral values among the students					
Day→	1	2	3	4	5	6
Value Orientation programmes	Story of American Swimmer Florence Chadwick	Story of King Asoka	Story of Chanakya	Story of Helen Keller	Story of Guru Nanak Sahib	Story of a Prince and his Guru

Week-7: Theme—Personality Development (Body, Mind and Soul)

Day→	1	2	3	4	5	6
Objectives	To motivate the students to become courageous	To enable the students to realize	To develop self-confidence among	To encourage the students for hard work	To develop positive	To inspire the students for social service

	and judicious	the omnipresence of Almighty	the students		attitude among them	
Daily orientation talk	In the last week, the investigator once again tries to club the whole package of seven weeks. Theme for the last week is personality development, which includes simultaneous development at the physical, mental and spiritual levels. There is emphasis on the three aspects—body, mind and soul—in the week. Through these steps, the investigator aims to inculcate confidence and values in the students, leading to an overall development of their personality.					
Yoga intervention programme	SAME SET OF YOGA INTERVENTION PROGRAMME OF WEEK 5 IS BEING FOLLOWED					
	The investigator through breathing exercises develops self confidence among the students. Sukshm Vietnam aims at the flexibility of the limbs and relaxation of the body. Padmasana helps the blood to run smoothly to the brain, thereby improving concentration and memory of the students. It also inculcates confidence among students and improves their academic achievement. 'Om' Dhvani creates vibrations in brain, which again improves its functioning. Gaytri Mantra promotes the connectivity of students with the Ultimate Power, i.e. Almighty, and enables them to be humble and polite. They get spiritual courage from the Supreme power. Suryanamaskar consisting of twelve asanas carries numerous benefits, which brings the students close to nature. Under this, they salute the Sun – Lord of Light and Brightness. Shavasana relaxes the whole self—Body + Mind + Soul. It also helps them to be one with the Ultimate and brings them to the state of nothinglessness. During this asana, the whole body is replenished and the mind too becomes stable. The practitioner is enabled to feel his heartbeat and the rhythm of his pulse, and thus becomes one with his internal body—complete oneness of body and mind.					
	Other set of asanas are useful for the whole personality i.e. physical growth, mental calmness and spiritual development. *Sarvangasana* is an asana for all parts of the body, which assists in the flow of blood to the brain. It also improves the working of the brain cells. *Pranayama* provides fresh oxygen to the body. It improves the breathing pattern and carries oxygen to each and every cell of their body. The complete pranayama package is extremely beneficial for the students as it makes them physically fit, mentally alert and spiritually strong. Meditation with the help of 'Om' chanting creates strong positive vibrations, which again provides benefits in abundance to the students. It improves the concentration of the students Prayer also plays a very important role in yoga. Prayer is recited at the end of the yoga session, which aligns the practitioner spiritually with the Super Power, i.e. the Almighty. Value orientation programmes are very much part of the complete package provided to the learner. The investigator takes regular feedback from the yoga learners, regarding their personal experiences of different asanas.					
Day→	**1**	**2**	**3**	**4**	**5**	**6**
Value-orientation programme	Story of Shri Vallabh Bhai Patel	Story of guru and his disciple	Story of Dr. Chandra	Story of Madam Marie Curie	Stories of two brothers and their father	Lecture on the Social activities done by actor turned MP Late Sh. Sunil Dutt

Findings of the Study

The findings of the present investigation are as follows:

- The students of 'Experimental Group' with yoga treatment yielded higher concentration levels than the students of the 'Control Group'.
- Those who practiced yoga module exhibited higher Short Term Memory than those students, who did not practice it. The students of the Experimental Group, who practiced yoga module, did better in their academic performance in Social Studies.
- The students with high stress with yoga intervention performed better than students with high stress and low stress without yoga intervention on the adjusted gain scores of academic performance in social studies.
- The students with low stress with yoga intervention performed better than the students with high stress and low stress without yoga
- Interaction effect of yoga and stress on the adjusted gain scores of academic performance in social studies was also found to be significant, which reveals that yoga intervention helped the students to improve academic performance in social studies by optimizing the stress levels.
- The students of experimental group, who practiced yoga module performed better in their academic performance in Mathematics.
- The students with high stress and low stress yielded similar levels of academic performance in Mathematics.
- The students of experimental group, who practiced yoga module performed better in their academic performance in Science.
- The students with high stress and low stress yielded similar levels of academic performance in Science.
- On the other hand, there was no significant difference in concentration, short term memory and intelligence between High Stress students and Low Stress students. But F-ratio computed was quite close to significant levels. Therefore, a much tougher investigation is needed to

measure its effect. The investigator too feels that stress affects concentration, short term memory and intelligence, which however cannot be discerned at very significant levels, whereas yoga clearly affects and improves concentration, short term memory and academic performance.

- A qualitative analysis was undertaken to assess the effect of yoga module on academic performance. It was found that yoga treatment has a positive effect on the academic performance of students in different subjects.

Educational Implications

The complete yoga module helped the students in improving their concentration, memory and academic performance in different subjects. Observing the extent of positive effect of yoga, it was suggested that it should be made an integral part of school education. Definitely the study undertaken has far reaching benefits for the school system as a whole and school children in the particular. Based on this significant research, further studies can be undertaken to highlight the importance of yoga to school going students, besides people in general.

Bibliography

Achenbach, T.M. and Edelbrock, C.S. (1978). The classification of empirical efforts. *Psychological Bulletin*, 85, 1275-1301

Agarwal, Manu; Nischal, AniL; AgarwaL, Anju; Verma, Jitendra and Dhanasekaran, Saranya (2010). *Journal of Indian Association Child Adolescent and Mental Health* 2013; 9(3):62-79

Agrawal, Rita (2001). *Stress in life and at work*, New Delhi, Sage Publications.

Ahuja, Rajneesh (2005). Delhi high on Dope. *The Asian Age*, July 22, p. 21.

Akhtar, Shameem (2006). Don't let stress bog you down. *The Asian Age*, March, 27. p. 26.

Alexander, A. Schneiders (1953). *Introductory Psychology*. Rinehart and Co., New York.

Alexander, C., Rainforth, M., and Gelderloos, P. (1991). Transcendental meditation, self-actualization and psychological health: A conceptual overview and statistical meta-analysis. *Journal of Social Behaviour and Personality*. Vol. 6, pp. 189-247.

Alexander, C.N.; Kurth, S.C.; Travis, F.; Warner, T.; and Alexander, V.K. (1979). Cognitive stage of development in children practicing the Transcendental Meditation programme: Acquisition and consolidation of conservation Department of Psychology and Social Relations, Harvard University, Cambridge, Massachusetts, USA, Hampshire college, Amherst, Massachusetts, USA, Department of Psychology and Public Affairs, Maharishi International University, Fairfield, Iowa, USA, and Department of Psychology, York University, Toronto, Ontario, Canada. Collected Papers V 4. 303.

Amato, P.R. (1990). Parental divorce and attitudes towards marriage and family life. *Journal of Marriage and the Family*, 50, 453-461.

Ameerajan, M.S. (1981). A schematic model of the determinants of academic achievement. *Journal of Education and Psychology*, July, Vol. XXXIX (2) 111-116.

Anderson, R.; Hiebert, E.; Scott, J. and Wilkinson, I. (1985). Becoming a nation of readers: The report of the commission on reading. Washington, DC: National Institute of Education.

Appley, M.R. and Trumbull, R. (1967). *Psychological Stress*. New York, Appleton-century Crafts.

Archer, J. and Lamin, A. (1985). An investigation of personal and academic stressors on college campuses, *Journal of College Student Personnel*, vol. 26(3), 210-215

Aron, A; Orme-Johson D.W. and Brubaker, P. (1981). The Transcendental Meditation programme in the college curriculum: a 4-year longitudinal study of effects on cognitive and affective functioning. *College Student Journal*, 15(2): 140-146. Collected Papers, V3. 261.

Ashcraft, M.H. (2002). *Cognition*. Upper Saddle River, NJ: Prentice Hall.

Atkinson, J.M. (1999). *Coping with Stress at Work*. New Delhi: Harper Collins.

Atkinson, R.C. and Shiffrin, R.M. (1968). Human Memory: A proposed system and its control processes. In K.W. Spence and J.T. Spence (Eds.), *The psychology of learning and motivation: Advances in research and theory* (pp. 89-195). New York: Academic Press.

Baddeley, A.D. (1986). *Working memory*. Oxford, UK: Clarendon Books.

Baddeley, A.D. (2001). Is working memory still working? *American Psychologist*, 56, 851-864.

Baron, Robert, A. (2004). *Psychology*, 5th edition, Pearson Education (Singapore) Pvt. Ltd., Delhi, India.

Basu, D.; Aggarwal, M.; Das, P.P.; Mattoo, S.K.; Kulhara, P. and Varma, V.K. (2012). Changing pattern of substance abuse in patients attending a de-addiction centre in North India (1978-2008). *Indian Journal of Medical Research*, Jun;135(6):830-6.

BBC News (2000). Yoga to calm pupils' stress, March 31, article available on line: http://news.bbc.co.uk1/hi/education/697084.stm

Beauchamp-Turner, Deborah, L. and Levinson, Daniel, M. (1992). Effects of Meditation on Stress, Health and Affect. *Medical Psychotherapy: An International Journal*. Vol. 5, pp. 123-131.

Benson, H.M.; Wilcher, B.; Greenberg, E.; Huggins, M.; Ennis, P.C.; Zuttermeister, P. Myers and R. Friedman. (2000). Academic Performance among middle school students after exposure to a relaxation response curriculum. *Journal of Research and Development in Education*, Spring, 33(3).

Berlyne, D.E. (1967). Arousal and reinforcement. In D Levine (ed.), *Nebraska Symposium on Motivation*, Vol. 15, pp. 279-286, Lincoln: University of Nebraska Press.

Berman, G. (1970). Psychological aspects of Academic Achievement. *Journal of Ortho-psychiatry*, April 1971, vol. 41 (3).

Berry, D.C. and Mcarthur, L.Z. (1986). Perceiving character in faces: The impact of age-related cranio-facial changes on social perception. *Psychological Bulletin*, 100, 3-18.

Berry, D.S. (1991). Attractive faces are not all created equal: Joint effects of facial babyishness and attractiveness on social perception. *Personality and Social Psychology Bulletin*, 17, 523-531

Beubel, M.E. (1977). Changes in cortical hemisphere dominance with Kundalini yogic breathing techniques. Unpublished Master's Thesis, Catholic University, Washington.

Bhala, Balmakund (1996). Yoga in Modern Medicine, *International Journal of Alternative and Complementary Medicine*, April, (Reprinted in Yoga and Health, August, 1996).

Bhatia, Chhavi (2008). Stress, peer pressure weigh on mind of adolescents. Expressindia.com, July 27.

Bhatia, Ranjana (2001). Stress management for students. *Journal of Indian Education*, Aug, NCERT, New Delhi.

Bhatnagar, Suresh and Saxena, Annamika (2001). *Advanced Educational Psychology*. Meerut, Surya Publishers.

Bhojani, U.M.; Chander, S.J. and Devadasan, N. (2009). Tobacco use and related factors among pre-university students in a college in Bangalore, India. *National Medical Journal of India*. Vol. 22; No. 6.

Bisht, Abha Rani (1987). National Psychological Corporation, Agra.

Brautigam, E. (1972). Effects of Transcendental Meditation programme on drug abuses. A prospective study—Department of Psychology, University of Lund, Lund, Sweden.

Briggs, J.B. (1962). The relationship of Neuroticism and Extraversions of Intelligence and Educational Achievement. *British Journal*, vol. 32, No. 2.

Brown, J.D. and Mcgill, K.L. (1989). The cost of good fortune: when positive life events produce negative health consequences, *Journal of Personality and Social Psychology*, 57, 1103-1110.

Bruning, R.H.; Schraw, G.J. and Ronning, R.R. (1999). *Cognitive Psychology and Instruction* (3rd ed.). Columbus, OH: Merrill.

Bryant, D. and Maxwell, K. (1997). The effectiveness of early intervention for disadvantaged children. In M. Guralnick (Ed.). *The effectiveness of early intervention* (pp. 23-46). Baltimore: Brookes.

Carlo, G.; Koller, S.H.; Eisenberg, N.; Da Silva, M.S. and Frohlich, C.B. (1996). A cross-national study on the relations among prosocial moral reasoning, gender role orientations, and prosocial behaviour. *Developmental Psychology*, 32, 231-240.

Carpendale, J.L.M. and Krebs, D.L. (1995). Variations in moral judgment as a function of type of dilemma and moral choice. *Journal of Personality*, 63, 289-313.

Chacko, R. (1969). Psychiatric problems in children. *Indian Journal of Psychiatry*, Vol. 3, pp. 147.

Channabasavanna, S.M.; Raj, S. and Kaliaperumal, V.G. (1990). Patterns and problems of non-alcoholic drug dependence in Karnataka, Department of Health and Family Welfare, Govt. of Karnataka.

Chauhan, Pratibha, (2002). Children's mental health panel soon, *The Tribune*, Nov. 30, p. 8, c-1.

Cheyney, Glenn, Alan (1983). *Television in American Society*, New York: Franklin Watts Co.

Childs, J.P. (1973). The use of the Transcendental Meditation programme as a therapy with juvenile offenders. Doctoral dissertation (abbr.), Department of Educational Psychology and Guidance, University of Tennessee, Knoxville, Tennessee, USA; Dissertation Abstracts International 34/08-A, order Number AAD74-03806.

Clark, J.M. and Palivio, A. (1991). Dual coding theory and education. *Educational Psychology Review*, 3, 149-210.

Collier, R.W. (1973). The effect of transcendental meditation programme upon university academic attainment. Department of English as a second Language. College of Arts and Sciences, University of Hawaii, Honolulu, Hawaii, USA.

Contractor, B.R. (1977). Intelligence and Educational Attainment, *Journal of Education and Psychology*, Oct, Vol. 35, No. 3.

Corliss, R. (2001). The Power of Yoga. *Time*, 157 (16) 44-53.

Cory, R. and Hufnagel, P. (1974). The effect of the Science of Creative Intelligence course on high school students. A preliminary report. American Foundation for the Science of Creative Intelligence, Hartford, Connecticut, USA, Collected Papers, V1.61.

Crooks, R.L. and Stein, J. (1991). *Psychology, Science, Behaviour and Life*. London, Halt Rinehart and Winston, INC.

Crow, A. and Crow, L.D. (1969). *Human Development and learning*, Eurasian Publishing House, Ram Nagar, New Delhi.

Crow, L.D. and Crow, A. (1965). *Adolescent development and adjustments*, New York, McGraw Hill.

Csikszentmihalyi, M. and Larson, R. (1984). *Being adolescent: Conflict and growth in the teenage years*. New York: Basic Books.

Cunha, J.D. (1995). We can not do it and better. *Famine*, Bombay, Aug, 25.

Datta, Damayanti (2016). 'Just Say Om'. Yoga Special. *India Today*. June, 27. p. 80.

David, A. Brent (1992). Suicide/suicidal behaviour. *Gale Encyclopedia of Childhood and Adolescence*.

Dhalve, H.S.; Lele, M.; Sharma, S.; Durge, V.; Tendulkar, P.; Nayak, S.; Kamat, S. and Thacker, P. (2002). Study of Depression in Junior College Adolescents in Mumbai: Discussion Forum, *Indian Journal of Psychiatry*, April.

Dhar, H. L. (1996). Veda in relation to human physiology and health. *Bombay Hospital Journal*, 38(2) 354-57.

Dhar, H.L. (1997). Meditation and Health. *Bombay Hospital Journal*, 39(4):738-41.

Dhar, H.L. (1997). Vedic Approach to health. Proceedings Benoytosh Centenary Issue, Nalhatl, West Bangal, 53-57.

Dhar, H.L. (1999). Research on meditation. *Bombay Hospital Journal,* 41(3): 505-7

Dhiman, Kuldeep (2002). Moral Thoughts. *The Tribune,* Sept. 07, p. 3.

Dora, K. Dallip and Nanda, K. Ashok (2003). Value-crisis in Academics: The way out, *University News,* 41(22), June 02-08.

Drever, James (1958). *Dictionary of Psychology,* Baltimore.

Dube, K.C. (1970). Study of prevalence and bio-sociable variables in mental illness in a rural and urban community in Uttar Pradesh, India. *Acta Psychiatrica Scandinavia,* Vol. 6, p. 327.

Dunham, J. (1976). Stress situation and responses, In National association in School masters (ed.) Stress in school Hemel Hampstead; National Association of School Masters.

Ebbinghaus, H. (1885). Uber das Gedachtnis. LeipzigL Dunker. (Translation by H. Ruiyer and C.E. Bussenius [1915]. Memory New York: Teachers College Press Columbia University).

Edmunds, G.J. (1984). Needs assessments strategy for back students: An examination of stressors and program implications, *Journal of Non-white concerns in Personal and audience,* 12(2) 48-56.

Erikson, E.H. (1950). *Childhood and Society,* New York: Norton.

Erikson, E.H. (1987). *A way of looking at things.* Selected papers from 1930 to 1980 (S. Schlein, Ed.) New York: Norton.

Eyerman, J. (1981). Transcendental Meditation and mental retardation. *Journal of Clinical Psychiatry* 42(1)35-36

Fehr, T.; Nerstheimer, U. and Torber, S. (1972). Study of personality changes resulting from the Transcendental Meditation programme: Freiburger Personality inventory. Department of Social Affairs, MIU/ Forschungsring Schopferische Intelligenz, Dormagen, W. Germany.

Feuerstein, G. (1990). *Yoga: The technology of ecstasy.* Welling Borough: The Aquarian Press.

Feurstein, George (2002). *The Yoga Tradition: Its History, Literature, Phiosophy and Practice.* MotilalBanarasidass Publishers Pvt. Ltd. Delhi, p. 82.

Fiebert, M.S. and Mead, T.R. (1981). Meditation and Academic Performance. *Perceptual and Motor skills.* 53, 447-450

Flynn. J.R. (1987). Massive IQ gains in 14 nations: What IQ tests really measure. *Psychological Bulletin,* 101, 171-191.

Flynn, J.R. (1996). Group differences: Is the good society impossible ? *Journal of Biosocial Science,* 28, 573-585.

Forbes, S. (2003). *Holistic education: An analysis of its ideas in nature.* Brandon, VT: Foundation for Educational Renewal.

Forbes, Scott H. and Robin Ann Martin (2004). What Holistic Education Claims About Itself: An Analysis of Holistic Schools' Literature. Paper presented at the American Education Research Association Annual Conference (San Diego, California, April). 26 pages.

Foris, Dave (2005). The effect of Meditation, UW-L. *Journal of Undergraduate Research* VIII.

Fox. E. (1993). Attentional bias in anxiety: selective or not? *Behavioural Research and Therapy*, 31(5), 487-493.

Freeman, F.S. (1962). *Theory and Practice of Psychological Testing*, (3rd edition). New York: Holt, Rinehart and Winston Inc.

Fritjof, Capra (1981). *The Turning Point*, Flamingo, An imprint of Harper Collins Publisher, London.

Gabriel, John (1969). *Children Growing up*, London University Press, p. 138.

Gagne, E.D. (1985). *The cognitive psychology of school learning*. Boston: Little, Brown.

Gangchen, T.Y.S. (1995). *Training Buddhist Self-healing medicine*: Buddha Centre, Jalan IPOH, Kuala Lampur, Malaysia; 3.

Gardner, L.P. (1947). Analysis of Children's' attitude to fathers. *Journal of Genetic Psychology*, 70, 3-38.

Garfinkel, M.S.; Singhal, A.; Katz, W.A.; Allan, D.A.; Reshetar, R. and Schumacher, H.R.J. (1998). Yoga-based intervention for carpal tunnel syndrome: a randomized trial—*Jama*, 280, 1601-1603.

Garrison, K.C. (1956). *Psychology of Adolescents*, Prentice Hall.

Ge, X.; Conger, R.D.; Lorenz, F.O.; Shanahan, M. and Elder, G.H., Jr. (1995). Mutual influences in parent and adolescent psychological distress. *Developmental Psychology*, 2: 406-419.

Gera, M. and Ahuja, M. (2001). Impact of classroom environmental and academic stress on achievement of IX graders. *Recent Researches in Education and Psychology*, 5(2) 20-21.

Goldberg, Carey (2005). Doses of Meditation Key to good health. *The Asian Age*, Dec., 4. p. 34.

Good, C.V. (1959). *Dictionary of Education*, (2nd ed.). McGraw Hills, New York., pp. 493-510.

Gopi Krishna (1975). *The awakening of Kundalini*. New York: Dutton.

Gottfried, A.W. (ED.) (1984). Home environment and early cognitive development. San Francisco Academic Press.

Grewal, Geetinder (2003). Self worth not by academic performance alone. *The Tribune*, April 8, p. 13.

Guilford, J.P. (1967). *The Nature of Human Intelligence*, New York: McGraw-Hill.

Gularnick, M.J. (ed.). (1997). *The Effectiveness of Early Intervention*. Baltimore: Brookes.

Gupta, Deepak (2005). Parents add to stress. *The Asian Age*, March 12, p. 11.

Gururaj, G.; Girish, N. and Benegal, V. (2006). The Bangalore study. Alcohol Control series 1. New Delhi: World Health Organisation,

Regional Office for South East Asia; Burden and Socio-economic impact of alcohol.

Hall, P.D. (1999). The effect of meditation on academic performance of African- American college students. *Journal of Black Studies,* 29(3), 408-415.

Hare, J. (2010). Holistic education: An interpretation for teachers in the IB programmes. A position paper of the International Baccalaureate Organization.

Heaton, D.P. and Orme-Johnson, D.W. (1974). The Transcendental Meditation programme and academic achievement. International Centre for Scientific Research, Maharishi International University, Fairfield, Iowa, USA. Collected Papers, V1.60.

Hendrickson, Gail (2002). Stress in adolescents. Encyclopedia of Diseases and conditions reported in Discovery Channel at www.discoveryhealth.com

Hindustan Times (2008). Smoke Bomb Ticking—Global Youth Tobacco Survey. March 20, p. 8.

Holistic Education Network (2011). Education with an Holistic Perspective. Tasmania, Australia http://www.hent.org/

Horrocks (1969). *The psychology of Adolescence.* Boston: Houghton Mifflin Co.

Houten, Van (2003). The Brain: Engineered for Divinity, an article published in *Ananda's clarity online magazine* March.

Hunt, R.R. and Ellis, H.C. (1999). *Fundamentals of cognitive psychology* (6th ed.). New York: McGraw – Hill College.

Husemann, L. Rowell, (1985). Social Channel TuneTV's effects. *Science news,* 14 September. 166.

IANS (2006). Change Teaching methods, exam system, *The Tribune,* Aug, 01. p. 13.

IANS (2006). Change Teaching methods, exam system, *The Tribune,* Aug, 01. p. 13.

ICMR (1984). Project report by the task force on multi-centre of patterns of child and adolescents psychiatric disorders (1981-83). Micrographed, ICMR, New Delhi.

Ingalls, S.I. (1984). The effects of superior intelligence and behavioural handicaps on the academic achievement and related attitudes of 5th and 6th grade Boys, (Unpublished thesis of University of Utah). D.A.I., Vol. 45, No. 9, A2836-A.

Innes, K.E. and Vincent, H.K. (2007). The Influence of Yoga-Based Programmes on Risk Profiles in Adults with Type 2 Diabetes Mellitus: 6.

Iyengar, B.K.S. (2001), *Yoga*: The path to holistic health, London: Dorling Kindersley Publishing Inc.

Iyengar, B.K.S. (2004). *Light on Pranayama,* New Delhi, India, Harper Collins Publisher.

Jain, S.C.; Uppal, A.; Bhatnagar, S.O. and Talukdar, B. (1993). A study of response pattern of non-insulin dependent diabetics to yoga therapy. *Diabetes Research and Clinical Practice* 19(1), 69-74. 1-1993

Jain, Shashi (2003). *Introduction to Psychology,* Kalyani Publishers, p. 249.

Jarial, G.S. (1981). Creativity, intelligence and academic achievement: their relationship and difference with reference to sex and academic subjects. *Journal of Education and Psychology,* July, vol. XXXIX, No. 2, 91-96.

Jarry D. and Jary, J. (1995). *Collins Dictionary of Sociology,* Glasgow: Harper Collins Publishers.

Jella, S.A. and Shannahoff–Khalsa, D.S. (1993). The effects of unilateral forced nostril breathing on cognitive performance. *International Journal of Neuroscience,* 73 (1-2), 61-68.

Jessor, R. (1985). Bridging etiology and prevention in drug abuse research. Etiology of drug abuse: Implications for prevention. CorylLarul Jones and Robert J. Battjes, eds. NIDA Research Monograph 56, DHHS Publications (ADM) Washington, D.C. 85-1335

Jhingan, Heena (2006). 'Helplines get frantic calls from students after Board results'. The Asian Age, New Delhi, May 24, p. 21.

Jiloha, R.C. and Sreenivasamuthy, R. (1983). Socially disadvantaged children. Is their mental health at risk? In Dube, S. and Sachdev, P.S. eds. *Mental Health problems of the society, disadvantaged,* New Delhi: Tata McGraw Hill.

John, P. (1980). Psychiatric morbidity in children: an Epidemiological study M.D. Thesis submitted to Bangalore University, Bangalore.

Johnson, L.D.; Malley P.M.O. and Bachman, J.G. (1985). Use of licit and illicit Drugs by Americas High School Students, 1975-1984. Rockville, MD: National Institute on Drug Abuse.

Joseph, S.; Sridharan, S.K.B.; Patil, M.D.; Kumaria, A.; Selvamurthy, W.; Joseph, N.T. and Nayar, H.S. (1981). Study of some physiological and biochemical parameters in subjects undergoing yogic training. *Indian Journal of Medical Research,* 74, 120-124.

Joshi, M. and Telles, S. (2008). Effect of four yoga voluntarily regulated breathing on memory scores. *Indian Journal of Physiology and Pharmacology* (in press).

Juyal R., Bansal R., Kishore S., Negi K.S., Chandra R. and Semwal J. (2006). Substance use among inter college students in District Dehradun. *Indian Journal of Community Medicine.* 31: 252–54.

Kagan, D.M. and Squires, R.L. (1984). Compulsive eating, dieting, stress and hostility among college students. *Journal of college students Personnel,* Vol. 25(3), 213-220.

Kahn, R.L.; Wolfe, Snock and Rosenthal (1964). *Organizational stress: Studied in Role Conflict and Ambiguity*. Wiley, New York.

Kalam, APJ (2003). *Ignited Minds: Unleashing the Power Within India.* Penguin Global, 2003

Kandel, D.B. (1980). Drug and Drinking behaviour among youth. *Annual Review of Sociology,* 6: 235-285.

Karasek, R. and Theorell, T. (1990). *Healthy work: Job stress, productivity, and the reconstruction of working life.* New York: Basic Books.

Keenan, K. (1998). *The Management Guide to Handling Stress.* New Delhi: Pustak Mehal.

Keller, E.D. and Rawley, V.N. (1964). The relation among anxiety, intelligence and scholastic achievement in Junior high school children. *Journal of Educational Research,* Vol. 58, No. 4.

Kember, P. (1985). The Transcendental Meditation technique and academic performance: a short report on controlled longitudinal pilot study. *British Journal of Educational Psychology,* 55, 164-166. Collected Papers, V4.306.

Kets De Vries, Mfr. (1979). Organizational stress: a call for management action. *Sloan management review,* 21(1), 3-14.

Khalsa, S.B. (2004). Yoga as a therapeutic intervention: a bibliometric analysis of published research studies. *Indian Physiol Pharmacol,* July; 48(3): 269-85.

Khosla, R. (1990). Psychological benefits of Vipasana meditation-a longitudinal pilot study of sixty individuals. Paper read at the international seminar on Vipasana meditation and health, Igatpuri, Nasik, Vipasana research institute in abstract of scientific papers, 11.

Khosla, V.; Thankappan, K.R.; Mini, G.K. and Sarma, P.S. (2008). Prevalence and predictors of alcohol use among college students in Ludhiana, Punjab, India. *Indian Journal of Medical Research* 128:79-81.

Kimura, H.; Ohno, S.; Kumano, H.; Kimura, K.; Kamei, T. and Toriumi, Y. (2002). Decrease in serum cortisol during yoga exercise is correlated with alpha crave activation. *Perceptual and Motor Skills,* 90 (3 Pt1): 1027-32.

Kindler, H.K. and Ginsberg, M.C. (1990). *Stress training for life: An Action Programme,* New York Nicholas Publishing.

Kintsch, W. (1998). *Comprehension: A paradigm for Cognition,* New York: Cambridge University Press.

Kirkwood, G; Rampes, H., Tuffrey, V.; Richardson, J. and Pilkington, K. (2005). Yoga for anxiety: a systematic review of the research evidence. *British Journal of Sports Medicine,* 39(12): 884-891, December.

Klaczynski, P.A. (1977). Bias in adolescents' every day reasoning and its relationships with intellectual ability, personal theories, and self-serving motivation, *Developmental Psychology,* 33, 273-383.

Klein, P.; Pilon, D.; Prossner, S. and Shannahoff–Khalsa, D.S. (1986). Nasal airflow asymmetries and human performance. *Biological Psychology,* 23, 127-137.

Kornhauser, A. (1965). *Mental Health of the industrial workers*, Wiley, New York.

Kotchabhakdi, N.J.; Pipatveravat, S.; Kotchabhakdi, N.; Tapanya, P. and Pornpathkul, S. (1982). Improvement of intelligence: learning ability and moral judgment through the practice of Transcendental Meditation technique. In Proceedings of the second Asian Workshop on child and Adolescent development, Bangkok and Bangsaen, Thailand, 15-24, Feb. Bangkok: Sri Nakharinwirot University. Collected papers V3. 265.

Kouzma, N.M. (2004). Self-reported sources of stress in senior high school students, Victoria University, Melbourne, *National Library of Medicine*, vol. 94(1), 314.

Kumar, Kundan, Yogacharya (2005). Achieve inner well-being through practice of yoga, *The Times of India*, Oct-21, p. 14.

Kundu, C.L. and Tutto, D.N. (1988). *Educational Psychology*, Sterling Publishers, New Delhi, Pg. 81

Lazarus, R.S. (1966). *Psychological stress and coping process*: USA: McGraw Hill Book Company, p. 147.

Lazarus, R.S. and Folkman, S. (1984). *Stress, appraisal and coping*. New York: Springer.

Lefton, L.A. (1985). *Psychology*, London, Allyn and Bacon INC.

Lewin, K. (1935). *A Dynamic theory of Personality*, McGraw Hill, New York.

Lewis, L.M. (1968). The relationship of achievement to reported self-concept and behavioural rating by teachers (unpublished doctoral thesis), Wayne State University DAI, 1971, Vol. 32, No. 1, 245-A.

Lindsay, P.H. and Norman, D.A. (1977). *Human information processing: An introduction to psychology* (2nd ed.). New York: Academic Press.

Lombardo, Thomas (2008a). "Ethical Character Development and Personal and Academic Excellence" http://www.centerforfuture consciousness.com/pdf_files/ Readings/EthicalCharDevWrkshp.pdf, Center for Future Consciousness, April.

Lombardo, Thomas (2011b). "Wisdom, Enlightenment, Science, and the Future" Science, Wisdom, and the Future. Genet, Cheryl (Ed.) Santa Margarita, CA: Collins Foundation Press , Fall (Forth coming). (http:/ /www.centerforfutureconsciousness.com/pdf_files/ Articles/ WisdEnlightScientFutFinal.pdf)

MacDonald, D.I. (1984). *Drugs, Drinking and Adolescents*. Chicago. Year Book Medical.

Mahaprajna, Acharya (2005). 'Effective management of five senses', *The Times of India*, Feb. 18, p. 12.

Mahatma Ghandhi (2014). Seven Dangers to Human Virtue. Quoted in Conscious Life News, 28 May. https://www.facebook.com/ consciouslifenews

Mantone, P.D. And Mayer, R.E. (2001). Signaling as a cognitive guide in multimedia learning. *Journal of Educational Psychology*. 93, 377-389.

Marie, D., Wyshak, G., & Wyshak, G. H. (2008). Yoga prevents bullying in schools. Available at http://www.calmingkidsyoga. org/Gifs/ YogaPreventsBullyingInSchool.pdf

Mayer, R.E. (1999). *The promise of educational psychology: Learning in the content areas*. Upper Saddle River, NJ: Preventice-Hall.

Mayer, R.E. (2001). *Multimedia Learning*, New York: Cambridge University Press.

Mayer, R.E. and Sims, V.K. (1994). When is an illustration worth ten thousand words? *Journal of Educational Psychology*, 82, 715-726.

Mckenry, P.C., Kotch, J.B. and Browne, D.H. (1991). Correlates of dysfunctional parenting attitudes among low-income adolescent mothers. *Journal of Adolescent Research*, 6, 212-234.

Mehta, P. (1969). The achievement motive in high school boys. New Delhi: NCERT.

Michelis, Elizabeth, De (2005). *A History of Yoga: Patanjali and Western Esotericism*, Published by Continuum International Publishing Group

Miller, G.A. (1956). The magical number seven plus or minus two: Some limits on our capacity for processing information. *Psychological Review*, 63, 81-97

Miller, R. (1991). Ed. New Directions in Education: *Selections from Holistic Education Review*. Brandon, VT: Holistic Education Press.

Miller, R. (2004). "Educational Alternatives: A Map of the Territory." *Paths of Learning, 20*, 20-27. [Online] Available: http://pathsoflearning.org

Miller, R. (2006). Educating the Child's "Inner Power". [Online] Available

Mishra, A.; Vankar, G.K. and Pandey O.P. (2002). A study of adolescent depression and abuse, Discussion Forum, *Indian Journal of Psychiatry*, April, 2002.

Mishra, A.; Vankar, G.K. and Pandey O.P. (2002). A study of adolescent depression and abuse, Discussion Forum, *Indian Journal of Psychiatry*, April, 2002.

Miskiman, D.E. (1972). Performance on a learning task by subjects, who practice the Transcendental Meditation technique. Graduate Department of Psychology, university of Alberta, Edmonton, Alberta, Canada. Collected Papers, VI.57

Miskiman, D.E. (1973). The effect of Transcendental Meditation programme on the organization of thinking and recall (secondary organization). Graduate Departmental of Psychology, University of Alberta, Edmonton, Alberta, Canada. Collected Papers V1. 58.

Mitchell, P.D. (1963). A comparison of the achievement – intelligence relationship of pupils with that of school systems. *Journal of Education Research*, 1963, vol. 57, No. 4, 175.

Mohan, J. and Bhatia, S. (1985). Intelligence, Sex and Psychomotor performance. *Indian Psychological Review*, vol. 28, No. 3, p. 1-6.

Mora-De, J. (1990). School related stress in Puerto Pican children, unpublished doctoral thesis, Dissertation Abstract Interventional, vol. 51(10), 3347-A.

Morgan, T. Clifford; Richard A. King; John R. Weisz and John Schopler (1986). *Introduction to Psychology*, 7th ed., McGraw Hill International Editions (for memory) Psychology series.

Morrow, K.B. and Sorell, G.T. (1989). Factors affecting self-esteem, depression and negative behaviour in sexually abused female adolescents. *Journal of Marriage and the Family*, 51, 677-686.

Motluk, Alison (2005). Meditation builds up the brain, 11:01, Nov. 15, Newscientist.com news service.

Murray, H.A. (1938). *Exploration in personality*. New York Oxford University Press

Murthy, P.; Manjunatha, N.; Subodh, B.N.; Chand, P.K. and Benegal, V. (2010). Substance use and addiction research in India. *Indian Journal of Psychiatry*, 52 (Suppl 1): S189-99.

Murthy, Srinivasa (2003). Rebuild community life to prevent suicide. *The Tribune*, April 30, pg.11, c-1 (Section OPED).

Nagarathana, R. and Nagendra, H.R. (1985). Yoga for bronchial asthama, a controlled study. *British Medical Journal* Vol. 291, p. 1077-9.

Nagendra, H.R. (1999). *Pranayama*. Vivekananda Kendra Yoga Prakashana. Bangalore.

Nagendra, H.R.; Mohan, T. and Shriram, A. (1988). *Yoga in Education*, Vol. 1, Vivekananda Kendra Yoga Anusandhana Samsthan, Yoga Research Foundation, Bangalore.

Naik, Anshuman; Patel, Shashikala; Biswas, D.A. and Verma, Manish. (2016). Effect of Rajyoga Meditation on Intelligence Quotient of Attention Deficit Hyperactivity Disorder. Journal of Yoga and Physical Therapy 6:2 http://dx.doi.org/10.4172/2157-7595.1000242 Research Article Open Access no. 1.

Narain, R.; Sardana, S; Gupta, S. and Sehgal, A.(2009). Age at initiation & prevalence of tobacco use among school children in Noida, India (ICMR), October 5.

National Crime Records Bureau, Ministry of Home Affairs, New Delhi, (2012). [accessed on November 15, 2012]. Accidental deaths and suicides in India 2011; p. 317. Available from: http://ncrb.nic.in/CD-ADSI2011/ADSI-2011%20REPORT.pdf

Nava, R.G. (2000). A multidimensional multilevel model of holistic education. Paper presented at the 8th International Holistic Education Conference in Guadalajara, Mexico, November.

Neisser, U. (1976). *Cognition and reality*. San Francisco. Freeman.

Neisser, U.; Boodoo, G.; Bouchard, T.J. Jr.; Bykin, A.; Brody, N.; Cesi, S.J.; Halpern, D.F.; Loehlin, J.C.; Perloff, R.; Sternberg, R.J. and Urbina, S. (1996). Intelligence: Known and unknowns. *American Psychologists*, 51, 77-101.

Neves, A.C. (2009). A holistic approach to the Ontario curriculum, *Dissertation, CAN: University of Toronto.*

Nidich, S. (1975). A study of the relationship of the Transcendental Meditation programme to Kohlberg's stages of Moral reasoning. Doctoral thesis (abbr.), Department of Learning and Development, College of Education, University of Cincinnati, Cincinnati, Ohio, U.S.A., Dissertation Abstract International, 36: 4361a-4362a.

Nidich, S.I.; Nidich, R.J. and Rainforth, M. (1986). School effectiveness: achievement gains at the Maharishi School of the Age of Enlightenment. *Education*, 107: 49-54.

Noshpitz, J.D. and Coddington, R.D. (EDS) (1990). *Stressors and the adjustment disorders*. New York: John Wiley.

O' Conner and Anne-Marie (2001). Inner-City students get 'om Schooling' in yoga. Meditation: Instructors hope free classes will help needy youngsters to find inner peace. *The Los Angeles Times*, October 30.

Offord, D.R.; Sullivan, K.; Allen, N. and Abrams, N. (1979). Delinquency hyperactivity. *Journal of Nervous and Mental Diseases*, 167, 734-41.

Omizo, M.M.; Omizo, S.A. and Suzuki, L.A. (1988). Children and Stress: An exploratory study of stressors and symptoms. *The school counsellor*, vol. 35(4), 267-274.

Orme-Johnson, D.W. (1992). Theory and research on conflict resolution through the Maharishi Effect. *Modern Science and Vedic Science* 5(1-2): 76-98.

Osho, Rajneesh (1997). *The Greatest Challenge: The Golden Future*. Sterling Pub. Pvt. Ltd.

Osho, Rajneesh (2015).'The Five Dimensions of Holistic Education'. In *The Greatest Challenge: Golden Future.*

Parikh, Samir (2005). Six suicides, 300 attempts, *The Times of India*, Feb 21, p. 1.

Parmananda, Swami (2000). Concentration and meditation, Madras, Sri Ramakrishana Math.

Patel, C.H. (1993). Yoga and biofeedback in the management of hypertension. Lancet. 2:1053-1055.

Patel, D.R. and Greydanes, D.E. (1999). Substance abuse: A pediatric concern. *Indian Journal of Pediatrics*. 66: 557-567.

Permananda, Swami (1996). Harmony through yogasanas and meditation, *The Indian Express*, Aug 22, p. 11.

Pershad, Dwarka and Wig, N.N. (1994). PGI Memory Scale, National Psychological Corporation, Agra.

Pestonjee, D.M. (1992). *Stress and Coping, The Indian Experience* (2nd ed.), New Delhi, Sage Publications.

Philip, J. Corry and Veena, Kumari (1998). Impulsivity, Times of Day and Stress Effects on intelligence Test performance, *Journal of Research in Personality*, Vol. 32, Issue 1, March 01, pp .1-12.

Piaget, J. (1952). *The origins of intelligence in children,* New York: International Universities Press.

Pilkington, Karen; Kirkwood Graham; Rampes, Hagen and Richardson Janet (2005). Yoga for depression: The research evidence. *Journal of Affective Disorders,* Vol. 89, Issues 1-3, December, pp. 13-24.

Plomin, R. (1997). Genetics and intelligence: What's new? *Intelligence,* 24, 45-65.

Pressy, S.L.; Robinson, F.P. and Horracks, J.E. (1959). *Psychology of Education,* Harper and Brothers. New York.

Rama, Swami; Ballentine, R. and Ajaya, Swami (1976). *Yoga and Psychotherapy: The Evolution of Consciousness.* Gleenview, III: Himalayan Institute, p. 111 ff.

Ramey, C.T. and Ramey, Sl.L. (1998). Early intervention and early experience. *American Psychologist,* 53, 109-120.

Rani, N.J. and Rao, P.V. (2000). Effects of meditation on attention process. *Journal of Indian Psychology,* 18, 52-60.

Rao, P.N. (1978). Psychiatric morbidity in adolescence. M.D. Thesis submitted to Bangalore University, Bangalore.

Rao, P.V.K. (1995). Yoga: its scientific and applied aspects. *Journal of Indian Psychology* 13(2), 1-12.

Rao, S.K.R. (1983). The Conception of Stress in Indian Thought. The theoretical aspects of stress in Samkhya and yoga system. *NIMAHANS Journal,* 2, 115-121.

Rao, V.N. and Parthasarathy, R. (1998). Student Psychological Health, *University News,* Vol. 36(3), August 24.

Rao, V.N. and Parthasarathy, R. (1999). Talk in out. *Health action,* Vol. 12(1), p. 39.

Raven, J.C.; Court, J.H. and Raven, J. (1983) Progressive Matrices and vocabulary scales. National Psychological Corporation, Agra.

Reddy, V.M. and Chandrashekar, C.R. (1998). Prevalence of mental and behavioural disorders in India: a meta-analysis. *Indian Journal of Psychiatry.* 1998;40:149–57.

Redfering, D.L. and Bowman, M.J. (1981). Effects of a meditative – relaxation exercise on non-attending behaviours of behaviourally disturbed children. *Journal of Clinical Child Psychology,* 10, 126-127.

Rees, W.L. (1975). Stress, Distress and Disease. The Predential address at the annual meeting of the Royal College of Psychiatrists, London, July 9, Pub in *British Journal of Psychiatry,* Vol. 128, pp. 3-18.

Rice, F.P. (1992). *Intimate relationships, marriages and families.* Mountain view, C.A. Mayfield.

Rodin, J. and Salovey, P. (1989). *Health psychology Annual Review of Psychology,* 40, 533-580.

Ross A. & Thomas S.(2010). The health benefits of yoga and exercise: a review of comparison studies. Journal of Alternative Complementary

Medicine, Jan; 16 (1):3-12 www.ncbi.nlm.nih.gov/ m/ pubmed/ 20105062//

Ryburn, W.M. (1956). *Introduction to Educational Psychology,* London. Oxford University. Press, p. 220.

Sachdev, J.S.; Yakhmi, R.S. and Sharma, A.K. (2002). Changing pattern of drug abuse among patients attending de-addiction centre at Faridkot. *Indian Journal of Psychiatry*. 44:353–5.

Sachdeva, V. (1994). The effect of yogic lifestyle in hypertension. *Homeostasis in Health Disease,* 35(4-5), 264.

Sahasi, G.; Mohan, D. and Kacker, C. (1989). Effectiveness of yogic techniques in the management of anxiety. *Journal of Personality and Clinical Studies,* (1), 51-55.

Sailer, H.S.; Schlacter, J. and Edwards, M.R. (1982). Stress—causes, consequences and coping strategies. *Personnel Psychology,* 59(2), 35 48.

Sandstrom, C.I. (1966). *The Psychology of childhood and Adolescence,* London, Methuen and Co. Ltd., pp, 149.

Sanyal, Sourav (2003). Children getting hooked to alcohol. *The Times of India,* March 1, p. 2, c.1.

Sapolsky, Robert (1998). *Why Zebras Don't Get Ulcers,* W.H. Freeman and Co., New York.

Sarason, I.G. and Sarason, B.R. (2000). *Stress, Coping and Maladaptive Behaviour, Abnormal Psychology,* Prentice Hall of India Pvt. Ltd. New Delhi, pg. 134.

Saraswati, S. (1987). Asana, Pranayama, Mudra, Bandha Munger: Bihar School of Yoga.

Saraswati, Swami Niranjanananda. (1995). Lecture at Defence institute of Physiology and Allied Sciences (DIPAS), Delhi, October.

Saxena V., Saxena Y., Kishore G., Kumar P. (2010). A study on substance abuse among school going male adolescents of Doiwala Block, District Dehradun. *Indian Journal of Public Health* 2010; 54:197-200.

Schaeffer, R. (2002). Sharpen your memory with yoga. Natural Health, 6, 40. Retrieved on August 15, 2006, from http://proxy.tamu-commerce.edu:2048/login ?url=http://search.epnet.com/login.aspx? direct=trueanddb=awhandjid=NHE

Schunk, D.H. (2000). *Learning theories: An educational perspective* (3rd ed.) Columbus, OH: Merill/Prentice-Hall.

Scott, W.P. (1988). *Dictionary of Sociology,* New Delhi: Goyal Saab

Seetha, B.C. (1975). An inquiry into the psychological and social factors affecting academic achievement, (Unpublished doctoral thesis), Banard univ. In: Second Survey of 'Research in Education, (Ed.) M.B. Buch. CASE, M.S. univ. of Baroda, 1979.

Selye, H. (1976). *The stress of life.* 2nd edition: McGraw Hill, New York

Sethi, B.B. (1967). 300 families, A psychiatric survey, *Indian Journal of Psychiatry,* Vol. 9, pp. 280.

Shah, A.H.; Joshi, S.V.; Mehrotra, P.P.; Potdar, N. and Dhar, H.L. (2001). Effect of Saral Meditation on intelligence, performance and cardiopulmonary functions. Indian *Journal of Medical Sciences,* Nov. 2001, 55(11): 604-608. PMID: 12508633.

Shariff, I.A. (1992). A study of psychological problems of young learners. Ph.D. thesis, Karnataka University, Dharmad.

Sharma, Rajnish (2002). Yoga for sports and health. *The Tribune,* Sports Feature April 6, p. 24.

Sharma, Vikas (2007). Is your child suffering from stress disorder? *The Tribune,* Feb. 21, p. 14.

Shecter, H. (1977) The TM program in the classroom: A psychological evaluation. Doctoral thesis (summary), Graduate Department of Psychology, York University, North York, Ontario, Canada, Dissertation Abstracts International 38(07) 3372B. Collected Papers V1.62

Siddhinathananda, Swami (2001). Meditation according to the Bhagvata, Paths of Meditation, Sri Ramakrishna Math, Mylapor, Chennai.

Sigman, M. (1995). Nutrition and Child development: More food for thought. *Current Directions in Psychological Science,* 4, 52-55.

Singh (1986). Trends of Medical research in Yoga, *Annals of NAIM,* Vol. I, no. 1 p. 59-77.

Singh, Yogesh; Sharma, Ratna and Talwar, Anjana (2012). Immediate and Long-term Effects of Meditation on Acute Stress Reactivity, Cognitive Functions and *Intelligence. Alternative Therapies,* Nov/Dec, Vol. 18, No. 6; (46-53).

Sinha, D.N.; Reddy, K.S.; Rahman, K.; Warren, C.W.; Jones, N.R. and Asma, S. (2006). Linking Global Youth Tobacco Survey (GYTS) data to the WHO framework convention on tobacco control: the case for *India. Indian Journal of Public Health.* 50: 76-89.

Sinha, N.C.P. (1967). A study of intelligence and some personality factors in relation to Academic Achievement of School students (unpublished doctoral thesis), Magadh University. In: A survey of research in Education, (Ed.) M.B. Buch CASE, M.S. University of Baroda.

Sivananda Yoga Vedanta Centre (1996). *Yoga, mind and body.* London: Dorling Kinsley Ltd.

Sivananda, Swami (1974). *Bliss Devine,* p. 78, published by the Divine Life Society, Himalayas, India.

Smith, K.B. and Pukall, C.F. (2009). An evidence-based review of Yoga: A complementary intervention for patients with cancer. *Psycho-Oncology,* 18(5):465–75.

Smut, J C (1926). The first publication of Holism and Evolution was by Mac Milan and Co. in 1926. Smuts published a 2nd edition in 1927 and there have been at least three subsequent reprints; Compass/ Viking Press 1961, Greenwood Press 1973, Sierra Sunrise Books 1999 (a version edited by Sanford Holst). The full text of the 1927, 2nd edition, is available on the Internet Archive site and this is the source used in updating the Holism page.

Srinivasamurthy, R. (1974). Behaviour disorder of childhood and adolescents. *Indian Journal of Psychiatry*, Vol. 16, pp. 229.

Srivastava, J.P. (1974). A study of the effect of academic and personality characteristics on the academic achievement of Boys reading in class X, (unpublished doctoral thesis), Rajasthan University. In *Second Survey of Research in Education*, (Ed.) M.B. Buch. CASE, M.S. University of Baroda.

Srivastava, Pallavi (2007). Article "Are we playing with our kids' minds?" Sunday, *The Times of India*, New Delhi, Chandigarh, Dec. 16.

Srivastava, S.S. and Verma, D.P. (1999). Effect of yoga education on students: An experimental study. *Indian Journal of Educational Research*, vol. 18(2), 37-54.

Stack, R. (2004) in Holistic Education Network, holistic education. http://www.hent.org/world/history/Holistic%20History3.htm handle: @drsteve44.

Steinberger, E.D. (1994). Improving Student achievement, Virginia, American Association of School Administrators.

Stephens, W. (1956). *The Study of Behaviour*. Chicago, The University of Chicago Press.

Steptoe, A.; Kearsley, N. and Walters, N. (1993). Cardiovascular activity during mental stress following vigorous exercise in sportsmen and inactive men, *Psychophysiology Journal*, 30, 245-252.

Stern, W. (1914). Psychological Methods of Testing Intelligence, Baltimore: Warmick and York: Inc., p. 3.

Sternberg, R.J. (1985). *Intelligence applied*. San Diego H.B.I

Sternberg, R.J. (1988). Triangulating love. In R.J. Sternberg and H.J. Barnes (Eds.), *The psychology of love* (pp. 119-138). New Haven, CT: Yale University Press.

Sternberg, R.J. (1999). *Cognitive Psychology* (2nd ed.). Ft. Worth, TX: Harcourt Brace.

Stice, E. and Barrera, M. Jr. (1995). A longitudinal examination of the reciprocal relations between perceived parenting and adolescents' substance use and externalizing behaviour. *Developmental Psychology*, 31, 332-334.

Stoddard, G.D. (1943). *The meaning of intelligence*. New York: Macmillan, p. 4.

Stratton, P. and Hayes, N. (1991). *Dictionary of Psychology*. New Delhi: Universal Book Stall

Subramanyama, S. and Porkodi, K. (1981). Yoga its probable role in maintaining and restraining normal health, *Yoga Review*, Vol. I no. 3.

Surya, N.C. (1964). Mental morbidity in Pondicherary. Transactions of AIIMH Bangalore

Swaller, J.; Van Merrienboer, J.J. and Paas, F.G.C. (1998). Cognitive architecture and instructional design. *Educational Psychology Review,* 10, 251-296.

Tacon, Anna, M.; Mccomb, Jacalyn; Caldera, Yvonne and Randolph, Patrick (2003). Mindfulness Meditation, Anxiety Reduction and Heart Dizs: A Pilot Study, Family and Community Health, 26(1): 25 33, Jan.

Tamini, I.K. (1961). *The science of yoga.* The Theosophical Publishing House: Madras, India.

Taylor, S.E. (1999). *Health Psychology* (4th ed.) New York: McGraw–Hill.

Telles, S.; Nagarathna, R. and Nagendra, H.R. (1994). Breathing through a particular nostril can alter metabolism and autonomic activities, *Indian Journal of Physiology and Pharmacology,* 38(2): 133-137

Telles, S., Nagarathna, R. and Nagendra, H.R. (1995). Autonomic changes during 'OM' meditation. *Indian Journal of Indian Physiology and Pharmacology,* 39 (4): 418-420

Telles, S.; Narendran, S.; Raghuraj, R; Nagarathna, R. and Nagendra, H.R. (1997). Comparison of changes in autonomic and respiratory parameters of girls after yoga and games at a community home. *Perceptual and Motor Skills,* Feb, 84(1): 251-257

Telles, S.; Raghuraj, P.; Ghosh, A. and Nagendra, H.R. (2006). Effect of Yoga on performance in a mirror tracing task. *Indian Journal of Physiology and Pharmacology,* 50 (2): 187-190.

Telles, S.; Ramaprabhu, V. and Reddy S.K. (2000). Effect of yoga training on maze learning. *Indian Journal of Physiology and Pharmacology,* 44(2): 197-201.

Telles, Shirley; Nagarathna, R. and Nagendra, H.R. (1998). *Indian Journal of Physiology and Pharmacology,* 42(1): 57-63.

Thakur, Anshu Kant (2007). Yoga as prescription for life style corrections, The Speaking Tree, *The Times of India,* p. 16.

The Asian Age (2005). Doses of Meditation—Key to Good health. Dec., 4, p. 34.

The Asian Age (2005). Yoga finds room in parks, five-star hotels. July 22, p. 22.

The Indian Express (2007). *Stressed-out types at risk for memory problems.* June 16, p. 14

The Times of India, (2007). Stress and Performance. Feb. 07, p. 12.

The Tribune (2002). Depression and memory loss. Oct 01

The Tribune (2002). Drinking during adolescence hits brain. Dec. 13, p. 11 C.3

The Tribune (2003). Youngsters highly stressed these days. A survey done by US Medical Research Coucil. April 07, p. 11.

The Tribune, (2003). Meditation: the best stress buster. May 18, p. 13.

Thorndike, E.L. (1914). *Educational Psychology* (Briefer course), New York: Columbia University.

Tjoa, A. (1972). Some evidence that TM programme increases intelligence and reduces neuroticism as measured by psychological tests. G.I.T.P., Amsterdam, The Netherlands. Collected Papers V1.54.

Tjoa, A. (1975). Increased intelligence and reduced neuroticism through TM program. Findings preciously publishing "Meditation neuroticism and intelligence: A follow-up" *Behaviour: Journal of Psychology*. 3: 167-182. Collected Papers V1.55

Torrance, E.P. (1965). *Mental Health and Achievement,* New York: John Wiley and Sons

Trendall, J.C. (1989). Stress in teaching and teacher effectiveness: a study of teachers across mainstream and special education. *Education Research,* 31, 52-58.

Tripathi, K.M. (1987). A study of personality and behaviour pattern profile in psychosomatic disorders and the role of certain therapeutic interventions, unpublished Ph.D dissertation, Banaras Hindu University.

Tripathi, K.M. (2005). Scope of Yoga for Refinement of Educational Process in Modern Globalizing World – certain reflections, Banaras Hindu University.

Trow, W.C. (1956) *Psychology in Teaching and Learning,* Houghton on Mifflin company, Boston.

Tsering D., Pal R., Dasgupta A. (2010). Licit and illicit substance use by adolescent students in eastern India: Prevalence and associated risk factors. *Journal of Neurosci Rural Pract* 2010;1:76-81

Tyler, L.E. (1974). *Individual differences: Abilities and Motivational directions,* Englewood Clifs, New Jersey: Prentice Hall.

Udupa, K.N. (1983). Yoga and Meditation for mental health in Traditional medicine and health care coverage, World Health Organization, Geneva, 134-41.

Udupa, K.N. and Singh, R.H. (1972). The scientific basis of yoga. *Journal of the American Medical Association,* 220, 1365.

Udupa, K.N.; Singh, R.H. and Yadava, R.A. (1973). Certain studies on psychological and biochemical response to the practice of hatha yoga in young normal volunteers. *Indian Journal of Medical Research,* 61, 237-44.

Uma, K.; Nagendra, H.R.; Nagarathna, R.; Vaidehi, S. and Seethalakshmi, R. (1989). The integrated approach of yoga: A Therapeutic tool for mentally related children: A one year controlled study. *Journal of Mental Deficiency Research,* 33, 415-421.

UNESCO (1996). 'The four pillars of education', in Learning: The Treasure Within: Report to UNESCO of the International Commission on Education for the Twenty First Century. Paris: UNESCO.

Vasudeva, Sadguru, Jaggi (2005). Chanting mantras can transform life. *The Times of India,* March, 17, p. 12.

Verma, Suman; Sharma, Deepali and Larson, Reed, W. (2002). School stress in India: Effects of time and daily emotions. *International Journal of Behavioural Development*, vol. 26, No. 6, 500-508.

Vivekananda, Swami (1973). Raja-yoga or conquering the internal nature, Advaita Ashrama, Calcutta, 280. pp.

Vivo, De, Marcela (2013). Benefits of Yoga, www.giantv.com/article/yoga-special-needschildren, March, 2, 2013.

Wagnon, M.J. (1937). *Readings in educational psychology*, New York: Houghton Miffin, P. 401.

Wallace, R.K.; Benson, H. and Wilson, A.F. (1971). A wakeful hypometabolic physiological state, *American Journal of Physiology*. 221, 795-799.

Wallace, R.K.; Mills, P.J.; Orme-Johnson, D.W.; Dillbeck, M.C. and Jacobe, E. (1982). The paired H reflex and its correlation with EEG coherence and academic performance in normal subjects meditation. Society for Neuroscience Abstracts 8: 537, 1982.

Wallace, R.K.; Orme-Johnson, D.W.; Mills, P.J.; Dillbeck, M.C. and Jacobe, E. (1980). The relationship between the paired Hoffman reflex and academic achievement in participants of the Transcendental Meditation (TM) programme. Department of Biology and Psychology, Maharishi International University, Fairfield, Iowa, USA.

Warner, T.Q. (1986). Transcendental Meditation and development advancement: mediating abilities and conservation performance. *Dissertation Abstracts International*. 47(8): 3558B.

Warr, P. and Wall, T. (1975). *Work and well being Harinonds worth*, Penguin.

Webster's New World Tm Medical Dictionary, (2008). 3rd edition, Wiley Publishing. Inc.

Wechsler, D. (1944). *The measurement of adult intelligence* (3rd ed.). New York: Williams and Wilkins, p. 3.

Weidman, A. (1983). The compulsive adolescent substance abuser: psychological differentiation and family process—*Journal of Drug Education*, 13: 161-173.

Whitman, Neal, A. (1985). Student Stress: Effects and solutions, *ERIC Digest* 85-1, Association for the study of Higher Education, Washington D.C.

Wilson, M. (2001). The case for sensori-motor coding in working memory, *Psychonomic Bulletin and Review*, 8: 44-57.

Woodworth R.S. and Marquis, D.G. (1948). *Experimental Psychology*, New York, Holt.

Woodworth, R.S. (1970). Contemporary Schools of Psychology, London.

World Health Organization (2011). Young people: health risks and solutions. Fact sheet no. 345. [accessed on June 8,2013] Available from: http://www.who.int/mediacentre/factsheets/fs345/en/index.html

World Health Organization. [accessed on January 15, 2013]. Suicide prevention (SUPRE). Available from: http://www.who.int/mental_health/prevention/suicide/suicideprevent/en/

Yerkes, Robert, M. and Dodson, J.D. (1908). The Relation of strength of stimulus to rapidity of habit-formation. *Journal of Comparative and Neurological Psychology*, Nov: 459-482.

Yogi, Maharishi, Mahesh (1993). Settled Mind, Silent Mind. An interview held by Kathy Juline published in Science of Mind.

Zutshi, Minna (2005). Exam fever—stress soars as parents fret, students lose sleep, *The Tribune*, Jalandhar Plus, March 04, p. 01.

WEBSITE REFERENCES

http://www.ncbi.nlm.nih.gov/pubmed/16185770
http://bjsm.bmj.com/content/39/12/884.full
http://www.gawler.org/cancer-and-mind-body-interventions-research
http://www.ncbi.nlm.nih.gov/pmc/articles/PMC2176136

Index